Social Security: Averting the Crisis

Peter J. Ferrara

This book was made possible by a grant
from the Scaife Family Charitable Trusts.

INSTITUTE

Library of Congress Cataloging in Publication Data

Ferrara, Peter J., 1956–
    Social security—Averting the crisis.

    (Cato public policy research monograph)
    Includes bibliographical references.
    1. Social security—United States. I. Title.
    II. Series.
HD7125.F468   1982   353.0082'56   82-14666
ISBN 0-932790-30-5 (pbk.)

Printed in the United States of America.

CATO INSTITUTE
224 Second Street SE
Washington, D.C. 20003

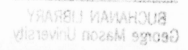

CONTENTS

ACKNOWLEDGEMENTS

I would like to express my appreciation to the Cato Institute for its continuing and seminal support of my work on this subject. Special thanks are due to Ed Crane for having virtually the patience of a saint, and to the many individuals at the Institute who contributed to the production of this book, particularly Kathy McBride for her careful editing. I would also like to thank Steve Savas for his encouragement. But most of all, special appreciation is due to Connie, whose support and affection make all things possible.

For Consuelo

The art of government consists in taking as much money as possible from one class of citizens to give to another.

Voltaire

Experience should teach us to be most on our guard to protect liberty when the Government's purposes are beneficent. Men born to freedom are naturally alert to repel invasion of their liberty by evil-minded rulers. The greatest dangers to liberty lurk in insidious encroachment by men of zeal, well-meaning but without understanding.

Justice Louis Brandeis
Olmstead v. *United States*
277 U.S. 479 (1927)

I. The Inherent Contradiction

Social security is the showpiece of America's welfare state. It is by far the largest of all government programs, constituting one fourth of the federal budget. It has enjoyed widespread popularity and support despite its controversial beginnings. It is the one program offered with confidence as an example of how government can improve the common good. It was the most important legislative act of the New Deal, and in the minds of many people it has come to stand for the New Deal itself.

Consistent with this role, social security has been virtually immune from serious criticism. Most economists have uncritically accepted the program's basic structure and method of operation. The program's many ardent supporters have refused to acknowledge any serious defects in the current system and have denounced the program's critics as enemies of the elderly and the poor. Some of the country's most respected public policy analysts have even labeled the program as among "the most effective and successful institutions ever developed in the United States."[1]

But the time for this Pollyanna approach to social security is over. In recent years prominent economists and other analysts have advanced many powerful critiques of the program based on its numerous serious shortcomings. Through its negative impacts on the economy alone, the program is needlessly costing Americans hundreds of billions of dollars annually. Young people entering the system today will never receive a fair return on all the taxes they will pay into the program over the course of their lives, nor will they receive as much as they could through private alternatives. The program remains in great danger of being unable to meet its future benefit obligations, despite recent tax increases and official assurances to the contrary. The program is fundamentally coercive, forcing virtually all Americans to participate regardless of their desires. It imposes a single insurance plan with one particular pattern of coverage and benefit provisions, instead of allowing a system of diverse options where individuals and their families could choose the particular plan best suited to their widely varying needs and preferences. The inequities and negative economic impacts of the system fall most heavily on some of the most vulnerable groups in society— blacks, the poor, women, the elderly, and the young.

[1]Joseph A. Pechman, Henry J. Aaron, and Michael K. Taussig, *Social Security: Perspectives for Reform* (Washington, D.C.: Brookings Institution, 1968), p. 1.

1

These problems have been compounded by the tremendous growth of the program in recent years. Social security has ballooned into what is probably the largest social welfare program in the world. Total expenditures under the program have grown from $10 million in 1938 to $38.4 billion in 1970, and $175.1 billion in 1981.[2] The program's total expenditures in 1981 constituted 25.5 percent of the total federal budget. Social security has now grown too big, and its many serious negative impacts have become too severe, for its defects to be ignored.

Many of the negative impacts of the program have become more severe in recent years not only because it has grown so big, but also because it has become so outdated. Social security was enacted in the depths of the Great Depression almost 50 years ago. Many of its features were structured to fit the economic and social circumstances of those times. Despite dramatic changes in these circumstances which have occurred over the years, there have been no fundamental changes in the basic structure of the program since its adoption. Many economic and social impacts that might have been thought desirable then are no longer desirable now. The Great Depression is over. It is time for social security to be reevaluated and fundamentally reformed.

An additional factor exacerbating the problems of social security is that the program has just recently begun to enter an entirely new stage of development. Social security operates on a pay-as-you-go basis. The tax money currently paid into the program is not saved and invested for the future benefits of current taxpayers; instead it is immediately paid out to current recipients. A crucially important but poorly understood characteristic of any such pay-as-you-go system is that it has two distinct phases of development—a start-up phase and a mature phase. Many of the most serious problems and shortcomings of a pay-as-you-go system appear in a powerful way only in the mature phase. America's social security system has only recently begun to pass from the start-up phase to the mature phase, and many of the most serious problems of the program are due to this development, which will be discussed in detail later.

The basic theme of this work is that the source of all the major defects of the social security program is an inherent conflict in objectives. The

[2]Social Security Administration, *Social Security Bulletin, Annual Statistical Supplement, 1980* (Washington, D.C.: U.S. Government Printing Office, 1982), pp. 83–86; Social Security Board of Trustees, *1982 Annual Report of the Board of Trustees of the Federal Old-Age and Survivors Insurance and Disability Insurance Trust Funds* (Washington, D.C., April 1, 1982), p. 56; Social Security Board of Trustees, *1982 Annual Report of the Board of Trustees of the Hospital Insurance Trust Funds* (Washington, D.C., April 1, 1982), p. 29.

current social security program attempts to pursue both welfare objectives and insurance objectives. But these two objectives are inherently contradictory and the result is both bad welfare and bad insurance.[3] The attempt to serve two functions with one program causes virtually all the program's serious problems.

Many critics of social security have focused on one shortcoming or another. Martin Feldstein has emphasized the program's negative effects on the economy through its impact on savings and capital accumulation. Milton Friedman has emphasized the program's negative effects on the poor and its compulsory, coercive nature. Arthur Laffer and David Ranson have focused on the program's financial insolvency and its negative impacts on the economy through the influence of the payroll tax on the labor supply. Edgar Browning has noted the political instability of the program. Warren Shore has illustrated how individuals can get a better deal in the private sector. As we proceed through this book we will come to each of these critiques, as well as several original ones, noting how all are produced by the conflict in objectives. We will therefore weave all the major criticisms of social security into this one unifying theme.

Our analysis also clearly indicates the fundamental reforms that are necessary to solve the program's major problems. The first step is to split the welfare and insurance functions into two separate programs or sets of institutions. The welfare function could then be performed by an entirely different program which could be more carefully adapted to fulfill the needs of the elderly poor, and the insurance function could be completely privatized. Individuals would be allowed to provide for their retirement and other contingencies by investing the money they would have paid in social security taxes in private insurance, savings, and pension plans. This would allow them to obtain the enormous advantages of private market alternatives to social security. As we shall see, these reforms not only flow logically from our analysis, but they are also simple and logical extensions of the major reform proposals

---

[3]The conflict between these two objectives of the social security program has been noted many times before. The conflict was explicitly recognized in a study published by the Brookings Institution in 1968 entitled *Social Security: Perspectives for Reform* by Joseph Pechman, Henry Aaron, and Michael Taussig. Recognition of this conflict was developed even further in a Brookings study published almost a decade later in 1977 entitled *The Future of Social Security,* by Alicia Munnell. See also James A. Buchanan, "Social Insurance in a Growing Economy: A Proposal for Radical Reform," 21 *National Tax Journal* (December 1968): 386 (Professor Buchanan referred to the program as "a clear example of a modern Buridan's Ass"). The two objectives are often referred to in the literature as the goal of individual equity (insurance) and the goal of social adequacy (welfare).

advanced by many prominent economists and analysts.

In advancing the criticisms and reform proposals discussed in this book, the goal is simply to improve the retirement prospects for today's young workers and to solve the economic problems caused by the program, while still maintaining the currently expected benefits upon which older individuals, for whom it is too late to make major changes in the program, have based their financial plans. This is a goal that persons from all ideological viewpoints should find laudable.

Despite the unquestioning, uncritical attitude that many have taken toward the program in the past, social security is like all other human institutions—it has its shortcomings, and improvements can be made through reasonable reform.

II. Social Security: A Background

Over the years, politicians and government officials have seriously misrepresented the social security program to the American people. These misrepresentations have been deliberately advanced to maintain the program's political support. But to understand the problems of social security and the possible solutions, it is necessary to understand the basic facts concerning the program.

Legislative History

Congress authorized the creation of the social security program with the passage of the Social Security Act on August 14, 1935. The bill established a wide range of programs that were meant to solve what was termed the problem of "economic insecurity," including provisions for unemployment insurance, aid to families with dependent children, and programs for the elderly.

We will focus only on the two major programs established for the elderly. The first, the Old-Age Assistance program (OAA), was primarily a welfare program providing immediate benefits to elderly individuals too poor to provide for themselves. The second, the Old-Age Insurance program (OAI), imposed a payroll tax on privately employed workers and provided retirement benefits for these workers at age sixty-five. This program developed over the years into what is known today as social security.

It is interesting to note the original legislative intent concerning the financing method for the OAI program.[1] The two alternative methods of financing social security are known as fully funded financing and pay-as-you-go financing. Under the former, the taxes of current taxpayers are saved and invested, and these assets, along with the accumulated investment returns, are used to finance the future benefits of these taxpayers. Under pay-as-you-go financing, the program's tax receipts are not saved and invested, but immediately paid out in the form of benefits to current recipients. Current taxpayers must then rely on the tax payments of future taxpayers to finance their benefits.

The original intent was to finance social security on a fully funded basis. Currently paid taxes were to be saved and invested in a trust fund large enough to guarantee all currently accrued benefit obligations. Future benefits would then be paid out of the accumulated trust fund assets. The program was to be operated on the same actuarial

---

[1]For a more detailed discussion of this point, see Peter J. Ferrara, *Social Security: The Inherent Contradiction* (San Francisco: Cato Institute, 1980), chap. 2.

principles used in private insurance plans. The choice of fully funded rather than pay-as-you-go financing was important in gaining public acceptance of the program.

The Social Security Act has been amended many times. One of the most important changes came in 1939 when Congress began to abandon the fully funded method of financing it had adopted in 1935 and to embrace the concept of pay-as-you-go financing. By 1939 the program had accumulated a relatively large trust fund. Significant benefit payments were not to begin until 1942, but significant tax increases had already been legislated for 1937 through 1946. The 1939 amendments, however, increased and accelerated the originally planned benefit payments, while delaying the scheduled tax increases, all with the express purpose of slowing any further trust fund accumulation. Increased benefit payments in fact started in 1940, and the tax rate stayed at 2 percent until 1950. The 1939 amendments also added benefits for dependents of retired workers and initiated the survivors' insurance portion of the program with the addition of benefits for survivors of deceased workers. Congress had thus begun to adopt the concept of using current taxes to pay current benefits. The process of changing over to pay-as-you-go financing, however, was not completed for several more years.

Another major amendment in 1956 established the Disability Insurance program, which provided disability benefits for workers under age sixty-five and imposed an additional disability insurance payroll tax to finance them. In 1965 another set of amendments added the Health Insurance program, which provided health care benefits for those over sixty-five and established still another hospital insurance payroll tax to pay for them.

In 1972 Congress amended the act to index benefits so that they would increase automatically with the rate of inflation and thereby remain constant in real terms. The indexing formula, however, mistakenly indexed benefit increases to both wage *and* price increases, which meant that benefits could increase at as much as twice the rate of inflation. This error threatened to bankrupt the entire system, and the 1977 amendments responded by "decoupling" the benefit formula so that benefits would increase at the rate of growth in wages before retirement and at the rate of growth in prices after retirement.

Financing

Since its inception, social security has been financed by a flat rate tax on payrolls; formally, half of the tax is paid by the employee and half by the employer. The tax is assessed only on wage income up to a certain maximum annual amount. The self-employed also pay a flat rate tax on their wage income below the maximum that is currently three fourths of the combined employer-employee tax rate for hired workers. Today, approximately 90 percent of all workers pay social security taxes.[2] Virtually all workers exempt from social security taxes, and not covered by the program, are federal, state, and local government employees. Most of these workers are covered by separate retirement programs provided by their government employers, programs that generally provide better benefits than social security.

The original social security tax rate was 1 percent for both employees and employers, a combined rate of 2 percent assessed against the first $3,000 of income. This rate continued until 1950, when the combined rate was increased to 3 percent. Today, in 1982, the combined rate is 13.4 percent assessed against the first $32,400 of income. The maximum tax has therefore increased from $60 over the first fourteen years of the program to $90 in 1950 and to $4,341.60 in 1982. By 1990 the combined rate is currently legislated to increase to 15.3 percent, with the maximum taxable income increasing each year after 1981 at the rate of increase in average wages. Based on projections of the Social Security Administration,[3] the maximum tax by 1990 will climb to approximately $8,700. (See tables 1 and 2.)

This expansion in social security taxes has made the program one of the federal government's largest money-collecting devices. In 1981 total social security taxes amounted to $172.3 billion, more than one fourth (27.6 percent) of all federal government taxes collected in that year. This was actually greater than total federal corporate and business taxes in 1981—$126.2 billion. Federal personal income tax receipts in that year totaled $296.2 billion. In 1982 total social security taxes were expected to reach $181.0 billion. (See table 3.)

The social security payroll tax has attained this prominent position among federal revenue sources only in recent years. In 1949 the program accounted for only 4.4 percent of federal revenues, and this portion had only increased to 9.9 percent by 1959 and to 13.8 percent by 1965. The program's increasing share of the federal tax bill is due to

[2]Social Security Administration, *Social Security Bulletin, Annual Statistical Supplement, 1975* (Washington, D.C.: U.S. Government Printing Office, 1977), p. 68.

[3]Social Security Board of Trustees, *1982 Annual Report of the Board of Trustees of the Federal Old-Age and Survivors Insurance and Disability Insurance Trust Funds* (Washington, D.C., April 1, 1982). Projections were based on the Alternative IIB assumptions in the report.

the fact that the program's revenues have virtually doubled in almost every five-year period from 1940 to 1980. (See table 3.)

Although the payroll tax is formally assessed half against the employer and half against the employee, the employee really bears the entire burden of the tax. Both shares come out of the employee's paycheck, just like employer payments for all other fringe benefits such as pension plans, medical insurance, and vacation benefits. Over the long run, the employer merely passes the full burden of the tax onto the employee by paying lower wages than he would have without the tax.

This occurs because an employer will never hire a worker if he has to pay more to do so than he will receive through the value of the worker's productivity. In response to the payroll tax, therefore, the employer will hire fewer workers, substituting capital for labor or simply reducing output, until the productivity of the remaining workers rises enough to pay for the tax. In this case, the wage of each worker will be less than the value of what he produces by the full amount of the tax. The tax will then be coming out of the value of what the worker produces, rather than out of the employer's pocket. Alternatively, workers might respond to the employer's reduction of his work force by bidding down their wages by the full amount of the tax in order to maintain their employment levels. In this case, however, the employee will again be bearing the full amount of the tax.[4]

An empirical study of the payroll tax by John A. Brittain also reached the conclusion that the employer's share of the payroll tax is borne entirely by the employee.[5] Brittain examined data from numerous countries around the world and found that wages in countries with higher payroll taxes were lower than wages in countries with lower payroll taxes by roughly the full amount of additional tax. Brittain concluded: "The essence of the finding here is that given the level of productivity in a country, the presence of a payroll tax on employees tends to reduce the wage in dollars by roughly the amount of the tax."[6]

Types of Benefits

Social security began paying benefits in 1937, sending out checks for $1 million in that year. From this modest beginning, social security has

---

[4]For a more detailed discussion of the incidence of the payroll tax, see Ferrara, *Social Security: The Inherent Contradiction*, chap. 2.

[5]John A. Brittain, "The Incidence of Social Security Payroll Taxes," *American Economic Review* 61 (March 1971): 116–25.

[6]Ibid., p. 32.

come to rival in total expenditures our entire annual budget for national defense.

The most basic of the program's benefits are the retirement benefits, available to all workers age sixty-five and over who have worked a minimum number of years. Retirement benefits are also available, at a reduced rate, to workers who have reached the age of sixty-two. Additional retirement benefits are paid if the retiree has certain dependents such as a spouse or minor children.

The program also pays survivors' benefits to the spouse and minor children of a deceased worker, even if the worker died before age sixty-two. A spouse without minor children, however, cannot collect full survivors' benefits until the age of sixty-five, although permanently reduced benefits are available at age sixty. The portion of social security paying these survivors' and the retirement benefits noted above is known as the Old-Age and Survivors' Insurance (OASI) program. OASI benefits account for approximately three fourths of all social security benefits.

In addition, social security pays disability benefits to workers who become disabled before age sixty-five, including supplemental benefits for the disabled worker's family. The portion of the program paying these benefits is known as the DI (Disability Insurance) program. The combination of this and the program described above is known as the OASDI program.

The final category of social security benefits involves the payments made under the Hospital Insurance (HI) program. HI benefits are available to all social security beneficiaries over age sixty-five, to disabled workers, and to disabled surviving spouses over the age of fifty. These HI payments are made to help defray some of the cost of hospital care and related expenses incurred by the program's beneficiaries. This and the other benefit programs described above are referred to collectively as the OASDHI program.

Social security benefits have always been exempt from the personal income tax. Since the employer's share of the social security payroll tax is not counted as part of the employee's income, it is also exempt from tax. The employee's share of the tax, however, is counted as part of the employee's income and therefore subject to the personal income tax.

In private retirement plans, by contrast, all of the funds paid in as contributions are, as a general rule, counted as part of the worker's income and therefore taxable. There are, however, numerous special tax code provisions, including those providing for IRAs and Keogh plans, that exempt at least part of these contributions. Also, as a general rule, the amount by which benefit payments exceed taxed contributions is generally counted as income and taxed when such benefits are received in retirement, although some private retirement plans could receive even less favorable tax treatment.[7] Federal tax policy, therefore, sharply discriminates against private retirement plans, as compared with social security.

Almost 90 percent of the elderly population in the United States now receives social security benefits.[8] In 1981 there were approximately 36 million beneficiaries.[9] In that same year, total expenditures under the entire OASDHI program, including administrative and other expenses, amounted to $175.1 billion. This constituted 25.5 percent or about one fourth of the entire 1981 federal budget of $686 billion. In comparison, federal non-social security transfer payments in 1981 totaled $109.3 billion, and federal purchases of goods and services in that year totaled $228.6 billion. In 1982 total social security expenditures were expected to reach $195.9 billion. This prominent position in the federal budget has again only been attained in recent years, with the past growth in total social security expenditures paralleling the increase in social security taxes. (See table 4.)

The Trust Funds and Pay-As-You-Go Financing

For each of the major social security programs, the federal government maintains a separate trust fund. The combined OASI and DI trust funds are referred to as the OASDI trust fund; and the combined OASI, DI, and HI trust funds are referred to as the OASDHI trust fund.

As table 5 indicates, in the early years the social security trust funds held enough assets to pay several years of benefits. As late as 1950, the OASDI trust fund held enough assets to pay over thirteen years' worth of benefits. Total trust fund assets relative to annual expenditures have declined steadily, however, so that in 1981 the OASDI trust fund held only 17 percent of one year's OASDI benefits, or about two months'

---

[7]For example, if an individual simply saved on his own for his retirement without taking advantage of some special tax code provision, the return on his savings would be taxed immediately when it was received. The individual would then not even have the advantage of having this taxation delayed until he received his retirement benefits.

[8]Social Security Administration, *Social Security Bulletin, Annual Statistical Supplement, 1980* (Washington, D.C.: U.S. Government Printing Office, 1982), p. 75.

[9]Social Security Board of Trustees, *1982 Annual Report of the Board of Trustees of the Federal Old-Age and Survivors Insurance and Disability Insurance Trust Funds* (Washington, D.C., April 1, 1982), p. 4.

worth. The OASDHI trust fund held only 25 percent of one year's OASDHI benefits in that year, or about three months' worth.

In order to guarantee all future social security benefits, the trust funds would have to be large enough so that their assets plus their investment earnings would be enough to pay, without any further future taxation, all benefits that existing workers and beneficiaries were currently entitled to receive in the future, without the accumulation of any further benefit entitlements. This would be the size of the social security trust funds if the government saved and invested each taxpayer's payments into the program and returned them with accumulated interest upon retirement.

This amount is calculated each year for the OASDI program by the United States Treasury Department. It is referred to as the unfunded liability (table 6). In 1981 the unfunded liability for the OASDI program was $5,858 billion or almost $6 trillion. Yet the OASDI trust fund held only $24.5 billion in 1981. Thus, the OASDI trust fund was less than 1 percent of the size necessary to guarantee future benefits. As table 6 shows, the OASDI trust fund has not been anywhere near this necessary size since 1967.

The social security trust funds, therefore, do not in any way serve to guarantee future benefits. In fact, with only enough assets to cover benefits for three to four months, the trust funds can hardly protect benefits against minor adverse developments. The so-called social security trust funds are thus little more than cash flow accounts where tax collections stop off only long enough for benefit checks to be written.

Furthermore, the low level of trust fund assets clearly indicates that social security taxes are not saved and invested to finance the future benefits of current taxpayers, but instead are immediately paid out to finance the benefits of current recipients. The program, therefore, now operates on a pay-as-you-go basis. As noted earlier, the original intent of the program, and the premise on which it was originally sold to the public, was that it would be operated on a fully funded basis. But, as table 5 suggests, Congress has perverted this original intent by raising the accumulated trust funds over the years to pass out free, unearned benefits, thus slowly changing to pay-as-you-go financing.

The Two Objectives of Social Security

With this description of the development and operation of the social security system, we can now see more clearly exactly how social security pursues two separate, distinct sets of objectives—insurance and welfare.

In an insurance program, individuals are paid benefits upon the occurrence of various contingencies. The amount of these benefits depends solely on how much the individual has paid into the program in the past, and the benefits are paid regardless of whether an individual really needs them. Thus, if a millionaire buys a life insurance policy of $1 million and designates his sole heir as beneficiary, upon the millionaire's death the beneficiary will receive the million dollars even though he also inherits his benefactor's other millions.

Social security serves an insurance function by paying benefits upon the occurrence of retirement, death, disability, or hospitalization. These benefits are paid under a formula that, in general, grants higher benefit amounts to those who have paid higher social security taxes in the past.[10] These benefits are, in general, paid regardless of whether the individual recipient really needs them.

A welfare program pays benefits only to the needy. The amount of these benefits depends solely on the degree of need; the benefits are paid regardless of how much the recipient has paid into the program in the past. A millionaire will never receive any welfare benefits, even

---

[10]All benefit amounts are based on the worker's Primary Insurance Amount, or PIA, which is determined by multiplying the average of past wages by the PIA formula. In 1978 the PIA formula was:

155.38% of the first $110
56.51% of the next $290
52.80% of the next $150
62.09% of the next $100
34.53% of the next $100
28.78% of the next $250
25.92% of the next $175
24.01% of the next $100
22.56% of the next $100
21.30% of the next $100

In 1979, an entirely new PIA formula enacted under the 1977 amendments took effect:

90% of the first $180
32% of the next $905
15% of the rest

The 1978 formula, with its annual automatic adjustments, was to continue in effect for some individuals in certain circumstances for a number of years. The 1979 formula is subject to annual adjustments as well. These annual adjustments are described in detail in Ferrara, *Social Security: The Inherent Contradiction*.

As these PIA formulas indicate, all benefits are a percentage of past average earnings, but since all workers pay the same percentage of their incomes, or at least the portion of their incomes counted toward benefits, in taxes, this means that higher benefits are paid to those who have paid higher taxes into the program in the past. The skewed weighting of the PIA formula, which undercuts this principle somewhat, is one of the welfare elements in the program. See footnote 13.

though he may pay thousands into welfare programs over the course of his life.

Social security serves a welfare function through the many elements of the program that result in the payment of benefits on the basis of need, rather than on the basis of past tax payments into the program. The result is that the beneficiaries of these welfare elements receive far more than what they have paid for on insurance grounds, while others receive far less.

One of the largest welfare elements of the program is represented by the start-up phase of the pay-as-you-go system. When this system was begun, taxes were collected from those working at the time, but there were little or no benefit entitlements belonging to those who were already elderly and retired, because they had paid little or no taxes in the past. Congress nevertheless used the program's initial start-up taxes to pay windfall benefits to the members of this first retired generation because it was felt that they were in need. These benefits therefore were paid on a welfare basis rather than on an insurance basis. As a result of these benefit payments, the members of this first retired generation received very high, above-market returns on any taxes they may have paid into the program, and to the extent that these returns were higher than market returns, they constituted a pure welfare subsidy.

The payment of these welfare benefits, however, is limited to the start-up phase of the program's pay-as-you-go system. Over time, new retirees will have paid more in past taxes, and their benefit returns relative to past taxes will fall. As the system enters the mature stage, new retirees will have paid taxes over all of their lives, and their benefit returns on past taxes paid into the program will have in fact fallen below market returns. At this point, the welfare subsidy will have been eliminated. The U.S. pay-as-you-go social security system is just now entering the mature stage, so the phase-out of this welfare subsidy is just now nearing completion. Nevertheless, one study has estimated that by 1971 approximately $370 billion in welfare benefits had already been paid to social security beneficiaries through this aspect of the program.[11]

Even though this welfare subsidy is coming to an end, without major reforms, its effects will be perpetual. Since the past taxes paid into the program were immediately paid out to finance unearned welfare benefits rather than saved to finance the future benefits of the initial gen-

[11]Douglas Munro, "Welfare Component and Labor Supply Effects of OASDHI Retirement Benefits," Ohio State University, Ph.D. diss., 1976.

13

eration of taxpayers, there are now no saved funds to finance these benefits on a fully funded or fully invested basis. As a result, the benefits of this generation, and all future generations, must now be paid out of current cash on a pay-as-you-go basis as well. Thus, it is because social security has pursued welfare objectives in addition to insurance objectives, and in particular the welfare objective of providing benefits in the start-up phase to those who had paid relatively little into the program themselves, that it now operates on a pay-as-you-go basis.[12]

A second major welfare element in the program is found in the basic formula for determining all benefit amounts, the PIA formula. This formula is heavily weighted so that those with lower past incomes will receive relatively higher benefits compared to their past taxes than those with higher past incomes.[13] Again, this is based on a welfare rationale. It is felt that those with lower incomes would not have adequate old-age pensions if these pensions were based strictly on past earnings or tax payments. They are therefore given relatively higher benefits solely because they may need them, not because they have paid for them.

Another major welfare component is the benefits for a worker's spouse, children, and other related individuals. A retired worker, for example, will receive higher benefits if he has a wife. He may have paid the same taxes as an unmarried co-worker, yet upon retirement he will receive 50 percent more in benefits. If he has dependent young children, he will receive still more. These benefits, therefore, are not earned by past tax payments. They are instead based on the welfare rationale that a retired worker with a wife and children needs more than a single retiree.

[12]It would be possible to operate a program with both welfare and insurance objectives on a fully funded rather than pay-as-you-go basis. The money from the invested trust fund could simply be paid out under a benefit structure with both welfare and insurance elements, instead of strictly according to how much each individual paid in, as in pure insurance. Therefore, the pursuit of both welfare and insurance objectives in the same program does not, by itself, require that the program be funded on a pay-as-you-go basis. It is, however, the program's pursuit of the particular welfare objective of providing benefits to those in the start-up phase who had paid relatively little into the program themselves that now causes it to be operated on a pay-as-you-go basis.

[13]As shown in footnote 10, the percentages of the PIA formula are skewed so that those workers with lower past earnings will receive a higher percentage of their past earnings in benefits than workers with higher past earnings. But since all workers pay the same percentage of their incomes, or at least the portion of their incomes counted toward benefits, in taxes, this weighting of the PIA formula also means that workers with lower incomes will receive more in benefits per dollar of past taxes paid than those with higher incomes.

14

This system of allocating benefits applies to disability and survivors' insurance as well. Two co-workers may have paid the same tax payments and may both die at the same age; yet if one leaves behind a wife with two grown children and the other a wife with two younger, dependent children, the latter will receive much greater survivors' benefits. These benefits were not earned by past tax payments, since both workers paid the same taxes. If both workers had paid these same tax amounts for term life insurance, both would have received the same benefit amounts upon their death. The greater survivors' benefits are granted to the second family because it is felt that they are in greater need, and therefore these benefits are justified on welfare grounds.

Still another welfare element is the minimum benefit provision, which provides that each beneficiary shall receive at least a minimum benefit amount, regardless of the amount calculated through the usual benefit formula or the amount paid in past taxes. This provision is again based on a welfare rationale—it is felt that any benefit below this amount is inadequate and that the recipient needs more regardless of whether he has paid for it.

The welfare elements we have discussed up until now all grant benefits to recipients because it is felt that they are in need, even though these benefits cannot be justified on the basis of past tax payments. But there are also several welfare elements preventing the payment of benefits that may be justified on the basis of past tax payments. These benefits are denied because it is felt that under certain circumstances the potential beneficiaries will not be in need.

The first is the earnings test, which reduces benefits $1 for every $2 that a beneficiary earns over a certain limit.[14] It too is based on the welfare criterion of need—the underlying rationale being that one who is earning over a certain limit every year does not need the benefits and therefore should not be allowed to receive them, even though he may have earned them by past tax payments.

The second is the maximum family benefit, which limits the benefits that can be received on one individual's earnings record to a certain maximum amount each month. This provision is based on the welfare-oriented premise that at a certain level benefits are no longer needed by the recipient, and therefore he should not receive them, regardless of whether he has paid for them.

[14]For beneficiaries between sixty-five and seventy-two, the income limit in 1982 was $5,000. This limit will automatically increase in future years at the rate of increase in average wages. Beneficiaries under age sixty-five are subject to the same rules, except that their 1982 maximum limit was $4,440. This maximum limit is also increased each year at the rate of increase in average wages.

Still another welfare provision along these lines is the one-benefit rule, which prevents a beneficiary from receiving more than one type of benefit even though he may otherwise be entitled to both. For example, a widow over age sixty-five who has worked all of her life must choose either the survivors' benefits on her deceased husband's earnings record or the retirement benefits on her own earnings record. Yet both these benefits have been earned on the basis of past tax payments. Her deceased husband paid taxes during his working years for survivors' protection, and his surviving widow would certainly have received commensurate benefits if the same money had been used to purchase term life insurance. In addition, she paid taxes during her working years for retirement benefits, and she would certainly have received commensurate benefits if she had been allowed to save and invest the same money instead. Social security, however, will deny her one of these two benefits on the welfare rationale that she does not need both.

There are numerous similar welfare-oriented qualifications and conditions on the receipt of social security benefits.[15] An example is the requirement that a widow under the age of sixty must remain single to receive survivors' benefits. Once again, the rationale is that in these circumstances the recipient does not need the benefits, and therefore they should be canceled regardless of whether the recipient has paid for them in past taxes.

To the extent that these limiting elements prevent the payment of unearned welfare benefits, they are merely an inefficient, ad hoc substitute for a means test. They do not precisely measure true need and consequently do not often prevent the payment of welfare benefits to those not in need. They may in fact prevent the payment of benefits to the truly needy. These elements, however, not only limit the payment of unearned welfare benefits, they often limit benefits that have been earned and paid for by past tax payments. They therefore serve an additional, independent welfare function within the social security benefit structure—restricting earned benefits on the basis of need.

These are the most significant welfare elements in the program, but there are undoubtedly others. Any element or provision in the program which distorts the amount of benefits paid so that this amount is not strictly related to the amount paid in past taxes may be considered a welfare element. These elements all serve to either pay increased ben-

[15]For a detailed discussion of these qualifications and conditions, see Ferrara, *Social Security: The Inherent Contradiction,* and Social Security Administration, *Social Security Handbook* (Washington, D.C.: U.S. Government Printing Office, 1980).

efits in circumstances where recipients are thought to be in greater need or to limit benefits in circumstances where they are thought not to be in need, regardless of the benefit amounts that may have been earned through the payment of past taxes. These elements, therefore, tend to cause benefit payments to be made on the basis of need rather than on what has been earned by past tax payments into the program.

It is thus clear that social security pursues both welfare and insurance objectives. As will be illustrated in detail in later chapters, these two objectives are inherently contradictory, and the result is to make the program both bad welfare and bad insurance. An immediate conflict between these two objectives should in fact be readily apparent. Insurance pays benefits to individuals on the basis of what they have paid into the program in the past, regardless of their need. Welfare pays benefits to individuals based on their need, regardless of what they have paid into the program in the past.

Supplemental Security Income (SSI)

In 1972 Congress overhauled the OAA program, creating the SSI program. Since its inception the OAA-SSI program has provided welfare benefits to the elderly poor, with recipients subject to a means test that required that they actually be in need before they received benefits. The program has also provided benefits to the blind and disabled below age sixty-five. The entire program has always been financed from general revenues, with the states providing partial funding until 1972.

In the early years, OAA was much larger than OASI. Considering just the old-age portion of OAA, the program paid out $244 million in benefits in 1937, while OASI, then OAI, paid out $1 million. In 1940 this portion of OAA paid out $450 million, while OASI paid out $35 million. As late as 1950, old-age OAA was still larger than OASI, paying out $1,454 million that year compared to $961 million for OASI. The next year, however, the OASI program surpassed OAA and continued its phenomenal growth while OAA remained virtually stable. By 1972 OAA was paying only $1.9 billion in old-age benefits while OASI was paying out $37.1 billion. In 1979 SSI paid $2.4 billion in old-age benefits, while OASI paid $90.6 billion in total benefits. (See table 7.) In 1979 about 9 percent of the aged population was receiving SSI benefits, about the same percentage as those in poverty in the general population.[16]

[16]Social Security Administration, *Social Security Bulletin*, Annual Statistical Supplement, 1980 (Washington, D.C.: U.S. Government Printing Office, 1982), p. 75.

Apparently, Congress recognized in the original Social Security Act of 1935 that welfare objectives were fundamentally incompatible with insurance objectives. It therefore enacted separate and distinct programs for each function. Yet over the years Congress has polluted social security with elements that belonged in a separate program such as OAA-SSI, if at all. The SSI program stands today as a ready, alternative vehicle for the welfare elements of the current social security program.

Legal Enforceability of Benefit Promises

Though a taxpayer may pay thousands of tax dollars into social security over the course of his working years and base all his financial plans on receipt of the promised social security benefits, he still does not have a legally enforceable, contractual entitlement to these benefits, as he would in a private insurance program. In the case of *Flemming* v. *Nestor* 363 U.S. 603 (1960), the Supreme Court held that the government has the power to renege on social security benefit promises despite the payment of past taxes in anticipation of such benefits by the disappointed beneficiary. The Court allowed benefits for the wife of a deported communist to be canceled even though her husband had paid the required social security taxes and she had otherwise qualified for such benefits. The Court said:

> To engraft upon the social security system a concept of "accrued property rights" would deprive it of the flexibility and boldness in adjustment to ever changing conditions which it demands.[17]

The Court also said,

> It is apparent that the non-contractual interest of an employee covered by the [social security] Act cannot be soundly analogized to that of the holder of an annuity, whose right to benefits is bottomed on his contractual premium payments.[18]

Justice Black described the meaning of the majority opinion in his dissent:

> The Court consoles those whose insurance is taken away today, and others who may suffer the same fate in the future, by saying that a decision requiring the social security system to keep faith would deprive it of the flexibility and boldness in adjustment to ever changing con-

---

[17]*Flemming* v. *Nestor* 363 U.S. 603, at 616.
[18]Ibid., 363 U.S. at 610.

ditions which it demands. People who pay premiums for insurance usually think they are paying for insurance, not for flexibility and boldness. I cannot believe that any private insurance company in America would be permitted to repudiate its matured contracts with its policy-holders who have regularly paid all their premiums in reliance upon the good faith of the company.[19]

Justice Black explained the majority opinion further:

These are nice words but they cannot conceal the fact that they simply tell the contributors to this insurance fund that despite their own and their employer's payments, the Government, in paying the beneficiaries out of the fund, is merely giving them something for nothing and can stop doing so when it pleases.[20]

Conclusion

In order to continue to sell the program to the American public, politicians and government officials have attempted to convey the impression that social security is just like a private insurance program. They have repeatedly told the American people that their tax payments are "pooled in special trust funds" where they are accumulated with interest and returned upon retirement.[21] They have suggested that the tax money supposedly paid into these trust funds guarantees the program's future benefits and the future security of taxpayers. They have contended that these benefits are legally secure earned entitlements and represent a fair return on past tax dollars paid into the program.[22]

The truth is that this contrived view is entirely false, as this chapter illustrates. Tax money currently paid into the program is not pooled in special trust funds but is immediately paid out to current recipients on a pay-as-you-go basis. It is not accumulated, it accrues no interest, and there is nothing to be returned in retirement. There are in reality no trust funds, but merely cash flow accounts where the money sits only long enough for benefit checks to be written. Tax money currently paid into the program therefore guarantees nothing about the future. All future benefit payments are totally dependent on the willingness of

[19]Ibid., 363 U.S. at 624.

[20]Ibid., 363 U.S. at 623.

[21]See, for example, *Your Social Security*, HEW Publication, N.(SSA)76–10035, June 1976. See also the sources cited in footnote 22 below.

[22]For a discussion of the misrepresentations concerning social security that have been advanced over the years by politicians, government officials, and ideological supporters of the program, see Ferrara, *Social Security: The Inherent Contradiction*, and Warren Shore, *Social Security: The Fraud in Your Future* (New York: MacMillan Co., 1975).

future taxpayers to continue to pay. These future benefits are not legally secure, and Congress can choose to revoke them at any time. The programs's benefit structure is riddled with welfare elements, and the actual benefit amounts paid are more dependent on whether one is married, the number of children one has, and their ages, than on past tax payments into the program. Taxpayers therefore cannot count on receiving a fair return on their tax dollars, and, due to the shortcomings of the program's pay-as-you-go system, virtually no one will be able to receive a fair return once the program fully reaches maturity, as will be discussed in chapter 4.

This chapter has presented the essential facts for understanding the program's many problems and negative impacts on American life that will be examined in later chapters. Our examination will also highlight the many reasons why the social security program must be fundamentally reformed. We will then advance a proposal for such reform in the last chapter.

III. Social Security and the Economy

The social security program has several important negative effects on the U.S. economy. As one economist has written:

> Because of the vast size of the social security program and its central role in the American system of financing retirement, it has major effects on all the significant dimensions of our economy. These effects are currently unintended, generally unperceived and frequently undesirable.[1]

With the tremendous explosion in the size of the program in recent years, these negative factors have now become too powerful to be ignored.

Savings, Investment, National Income, and Economic Growth

The most important negative economic effects of social security are due to the operation of the program on a pay-as-you-go basis. Because of this method of operation, the program causes a massive decline in total national savings, which in turn causes an equally serious decline in the nation's capital supply. The loss of this capital further results in sharp declines in national income and economic growth. The most forceful proponent of this criticism of the program has been Martin Feldstein, Harvard professor of economics and president of the National Bureau of Economic Research. His econometrics studies empirically demonstrate that social security does indeed have a powerful negative impact on these key aspects of the economy.

To see how savings are reduced, consider the individual worker who logically views his social security taxes as an alternative to retirement savings. The program's taxes consume the percentage of the worker's income that he would otherwise have available for such savings, and they finance benefits that serve the same function that retirement savings would otherwise serve. Therefore, the worker believes that he is in effect saving for his retirement by paying his social security taxes. He will consequently tend to reduce his retirement savings by the amounts he pays in such taxes.

If social security were run on a fully funded basis, each taxpayer's payments into the program would be saved to finance his later benefits, and there would be no net reduction in total national savings. Since

---

[1]Martin Feldstein, "Toward a Reform of Social Security," *Public Interest*, Summer 1975, p. 75.

social security is run on a pay-as-you-go basis, however, these taxes are not saved, but immediately paid out to finance current benefits. As a result, the program does not accumulate any offsetting, compensatory savings to counterbalance the decline in private, individual savings.

In 1981 total social security taxes amounted to $172.3 billion. Personal savings in that year totaled $106.6 billion, and corporate savings totaled $49.5 billion, for total private savings of $156.1 billion.[2] If social security caused a reduction in personal savings equivalent to the full amount of taxes paid, total potential private savings in 1981 of $328.4 billion would have been reduced by over 50 percent.

The reduction in savings caused by social security can be seen in another way. The individual worker may focus on the program's benefits rather than taxes and reason that he no longer needs to save for the portion of his retirement income that will be provided by these benefits. He will therefore reduce his retirement savings by the full, present discounted value of these benefits.

Again, because social security operates on a pay-as-you-go basis, the program does not accumulate any offsetting, compensatory savings to counterbalance this decline. The result is that total saved wealth will decrease by the full amount of the total present value of promised social security benefits. Feldstein defines this total present value as social security "wealth." This "wealth" does not actually exist anywhere in the economy. It is not real wealth represented by any real, tangible assets. It is merely an implicit promise that the next generation will tax itself to pay currently promised benefits. To the extent that this promise is reliable, however, it is perfectly rational for each individual household to regard this social security wealth as if it were part of the household's personal real wealth.

The amount of this social security wealth can therefore be used as an estimate of the effect of social security in reducing the total private stock of real wealth saved over time. Feldstein has estimated the 1971 value of this social security wealth at $2 trillion.[3] Total private wealth of households in 1971 was $3 trillion. Thus Feldstein's calculation suggests that social security may have reduced the private wealth stock, or private savings accumulated over time, from $5 trillion to $3 trillion, or 40 percent. This reduction in private savings is similar to the estimate

[2]Council of Economic Advisers, *1982 Annual Economic Report of the President* (Washington, D.C.: U.S. Government Printing Office, 1982).

[3]Martin Feldstein, "Social Security, Induced Retirement and Aggregate Capital Accumulation," *Journal of Political Economy* 82 (September/October 1974).

derived by viewing social security taxes as an alternative to retirement savings.[4]

Feldstein bases his contention that social security reduces private savings on these two arguments, focusing first on taxes, and then on benefits.[5] His econometric studies of past savings patterns and behavior empirically support this theoretical analysis. In a study of aggregate, national savings in the United States since 1929, Feldstein concluded that social security reduced personal savings in 1971 by between $40 and $60 billion as compared to an actual level of personal savings in 1971 of $61 billion.[6] This suggests that social security reduced personal savings by between 40 and 50 percent and total private savings, including corporate savings, by between 32 and 42 percent.

In a recent study, two Social Security Administration economists uncovered a computer programming error in this Feldstein study.[7] After correcting for this error, they concluded that the historical pattern of U.S. savings behavior provided no empirical support for the contention that social security substantially reduces private savings. Yet Feldstein had some problems of his own with the analysis of these two economists, and in a later study, after correcting for the programming error and updating the analysis to include more recent data, he concluded that social security had reduced total private savings by about 37 percent, which confirmed his earlier conclusion.[8]

Similarly, in another study examining the savings behavior of individual households, Feldstein concluded that individual households reduced their private savings by almost one dollar for every dollar in

[4]In a more recent and detailed study, Feldstein estimated social security wealth in 1972 at $1.85 trillion, using the most conservative assumptions. Compared to the 1972 total financial net worth of the household sector, $2.4 trillion, it again implies a reduction in private savings of about 40 percent. Compared to total private wealth of households in 1972 of $4 trillion, it implies a reduction in private savings of 32 percent. See Martin Feldstein and Anthony Pellechio, "Social Security Wealth: The Impact of Alternative Inflation Adjustments," Conference on Financing Social Security (Washington, D.C.: American Enterprise Institute, 1977).

[5]See Feldstein, *Public Interest.*

[6]Feldstein, "Social Security, Induced Retirement and Aggregate Capital Accumulation."

[7]Dean R. Seimer and Selig D. Lesnoy, "Social Security and Private Savings: A Reexamination of the Time Series Evidence Using Alternative Social Security Wealth Variables" (paper presented at the Ninety-Third Annual Meeting of the American Economics Association, Denver, Colo., Sept. 6, 1980).

[8]Martin Feldstein, "Social Security, Induced Retirement and Aggregate Capital Accumulation: A Correction and Updating." Mimeograph, 1980, written for Harvard University and the National Bureau of Economic Research in Cambridge, Massachusetts.

the present value of expected future social security benefits.[9] In yet another study, Feldstein examined international savings data and compared it with the various social security programs in different countries.[10] He concluded that countries with higher social security benefits and more complete coverage of the population by a social security program had lower rates of private savings.

Feldstein's empirical studies suggest that social security reduces private savings by close to 40 percent. The immediate effect of reduced savings is a reduced stock of capital. It is savings alone that provides the resources for the nation's capital investment. There has been much talk in recent years about a capital shortage. The heavy burdens of taxation and government regulation have slowed this country's investment in new capital equipment with the result that America today has one of the lowest rates of per-capita investment among the world's developed countries. Whether this phenomenon is referred to as a capital shortage or a capital crisis or by some other phrase, the truth is that capital investment in the American economy is vitally needed. It is needed to finance the discovery and development of new energy resources. It is needed to build new homes, to finance construction to revitalize our urban centers, to finance the creation of new jobs and upgrade existing ones. It is needed to modernize our factories to enable them to compete with foreign producers and to improve the productivity of American workers. It is needed to finance the development of new technologies, of anti-pollution equipment and better medical equipment. In short, it is necessary to finance the production of all the goods and services that Americans want to improve the quality of their lives.

The importance of the loss of this enormous amount of capital investment can be seen in the impact of this loss on national income and economic growth. With less capital, less of the nation's resources are devoted to production and to the materials necessary to increase that production. The result is less production and lower levels of national income and economic growth. By Feldstein's calculation, if social security reduces savings by 35 percent, then the long-run capital stock

---

[9]Martin Feldstein and Anthony Pellechio, "Social Security and Household Wealth Accumulation: New Microeconometric Evidence," Harvard Institute of Economic Research, Discussion Paper no. 530, January 1977.

[10]Martin Feldstein, "Social Security and Private Savings, International Evidence in an Extended Life Cycle Model," Harvard Institute of Economic Research, Discussion Paper no. 361, May 1974.

without social security would be 80 percent higher than it is today.[11] With this additional capital, Feldstein calculates that GNP would be 19 percent higher each year.[12] In 1981, then, in the absence of social security, GNP would have been increased by $550 billion. This was about 30 percent of total consumer spending in that year, almost twice the total of individual income tax payments and substantially more than three times the level of national defense expenditures. It amounted to $2,400 per person and $6,600 per family. Over the five years from 1977 to 1981, this aspect of the program alone needlessly cost the American people over $2¼ trillion in lost GNP. This total loss amounted to approximately $10,000 per person and $27,000 per family. This is what is meant when it is said that the negative impacts of social security have become too serious to be ignored. In discussing this disastrous impact on national income, Feldstein says:

> Let me emphasize that this lower level of GNP reflects the pay-as-you-go nature of our social security system. It is because social security taxes are used to pay concurrent benefits that the capital stock is smaller and income is less than it would otherwise be.[13]

This loss of national income, as well as savings and capital investment, is only likely to get much worse as the huge tax burdens in future years take their toll.

Criticisms. There is indeed considerable controversy in the economics profession over the magnitude of Feldstein's estimates of the impact of social security on the savings supply. Several economists have contended that social security has countervailing effects that tend to increase savings, offsetting the negative effect emphasized by Feldstein.[14] In

[11]Martin Feldstein,"Social Insurance," Harvard Institute of Economic Research, Discussion Paper no. 477, May 1976, p. 33.

[12]Ibid.

[13]Ibid, p. 32.

[14]Alicia H. Munnell, assistant vice-president of the Federal Reserve Bank of Boston, is primarily associated with the theoretical development of the "retirement effect." Under this effect, social security induces individuals to retire earlier through the earnings test, which cuts off benefits to those who continue working after sixty-five. The individual will then also be induced to increase his savings so that he will have enough assets to supplement his social security benefits during the additional retirement years and reach his desired consumption level in retirement. See Alicia H. Munnell, "The Impact of Social Security on Personal Savings," *National Tax Journal* 27 (December 1974:553–67; and Munnell, *The Future of Social Security* (Washington, D.C.: Brookings Institution, 1977).

Robert Barro, professor of economics at the University of Rochester, has suggested that social security tends to increase savings through a "full bequest effect." Under this effect,

fact, Feldstein himself recognizes the purely theoretical validity of these countervailing effects, but argues that his empirical work shows that as a practical matter these effects are small compared to reduced savings. The empirical work of Feldstein's critics, however, suggests that these effects are much greater; they find the net impact of social security on private savings to be much smaller than suggested by Feldstein.

Aside from the various econometric controversies underlying these differences, the problem with the work of Feldstein's critics is that the countervailing effects on which they rely are so highly implausible.[15]

---

parents would increase savings over their lives so that they could leave a large inheritance to their children to offset the transfer from children to parents imposed by social security. Parents would do this, Barro contends, so that they could leave the full net inheritance that they would have intended to leave in the absence of social security. See Robert J. Barro, "Are Government Bonds Net Wealth?" *Journal of Political Economy* 82 (November/December 1974):1095–1117.

Barro has also suggested that in the absence of social security individuals would not save for their retirement, but instead would merely rely on direct transfers in retirement from their working children. Social security would then have no effect in decreasing savings but would merely replace a private pay-as-you-go system with a public pay-as-you-go system. See Barro, *The Impact of Social Security on Private Savings* (Washington, D.C.: American Enterprise Institute, 1977).

See also Michael E. Darby, *The Effects of Social Security on Income and the Capital Stock* (Washington, D.C.: American Enterprise Institute, 1979).

In these writings the effect emphasized by Feldstein that tends to reduce savings is referred to as the "asset-substitution effect."

[15]See footnote 13 for a description of the various effects.

The retirement effect is entirely dependent on the earnings test, which is the source of social security's impact in inducing retirement. It is hard to believe that this test is responsible for inducing the $100 to $150 billion a year in additional savings necessary to overcome Feldstein's asset-substitution effect. In any event, the test has been weakened in recent years and soon may be phased out altogether.

Moreover, the retirement effect stimulates savings only among the portion of the population that is induced to retire earlier and only for the additional years of induced retirement and for the difference between social security benefits and the desired level of retirement consumption during these years. Feldstein's asset-substitution effect, by contrast, applies to the entire population, for all the years of retirement not induced by social security and for the entire amount of social security benefits during these years. This is likely to be a far more powerful effect than the retirement effect.

Barro's full bequest theory is based on a clearly erroneous assumption about individual preferences—that parents believe they need to offset the transfer to them from their children that is imposed by social security. The very existence and past popularity of social security indicates that most individuals believe that the program's transfer from children to parents should be made, perhaps in compensation for the transfers made from parents in raising the children. There is clearly no widespread belief that people need to save to offset the transfers made by social security.

Moreover, Barro's theory is highly implausible as a historical matter. When social security was first imposed, it immediately began a transfer from the first generation of workers to their parents, the first generation of retirees. Since these early recipients were

Econometric work is useless unless there is a plausible theoretical analysis to justify the results. Without such a foundation, the econometric results may simply be due to the inability of the analysis to separate out the impact of social security from the mass of real-world data and complex web of real-world factors. This is especially true when competing econometric work reaches different conclusions that are theoretically quite plausible, as is the case here.

Ultimately, however, this whole econometric controversy misses the point, because the important public policy question is one of opportunity cost. If the current, pay-as-you-go social security system were replaced with a private, fully funded system, there would be increases in savings, capital, national income, and economic growth of the magnitude suggested by Feldstein. Social security thus entails a significant opportunity cost.

Viewed in these terms, the immediate issue is not whether Americans

---

already retired with no other unplanned source of income, they could have saved to offset this transfer only by saving the social security benefits themselves and leaving them to their children. But we know as a historical fact that this first generation of retirees, who were generally considered relatively poor and whose basic needs the social security benefits were considered inadequate, did not save their social security benefits, but spent them on basic necessities. The first working generation, or second retired generation, would not feel compelled to offset social security transfers from their children to them, since this would merely be compensation for their own initial transfer to their parents. The same would apply to all future generations. So Barro's full bequest saving would never occur.

The only marginally plausible theory under which social security's negative impact on savings might be voided is Barro's suggestion that without social security, individuals would not save for their retirement but would support their retired parents with direct cash payments, relying on their children for such support in their own old age. But individuals today primarily supplement social security through savings and pension plans rather than through such direct payments, and without social security it is likely they would continue to rely on the same preferred alternatives in providing their full retirement incomes. The savings and investment approach has several decisive advantages over the private, pay-as-you-go approach; this explains the apparently widespread preference. The earned returns would allow individuals to have much higher benefits at a much lower cost, and retirees would have much greater control and security rather than relying on their children. Sociologically, the invested approach is much better suited to the modern American family, with fewer children to support parents and weaker links among family members.

All three of these countervailing effects are likely to have far less force in the future, especially if the proposal in the last chapter is enacted. In addition, even if these countervailing effects were sufficient to overcome social security's negative impact on savings, the ultimate policy conclusion that the program should be reformed along the lines suggested in the last chapter would not be changed. Only some of the reasons would be different. All of these arguments are discussed in greater detail in chapter 3 of my *Social Security: The Inherent Contradiction* (San Francisco: Cato Institute, 1980).

in the absence of social security would have saved as much as they pay into the program now, but whether it is worth saving and investing, through a private, fully funded system, the huge sums that are now paid into social security, considering the large investment returns that would result from a private system. The resulting large increases in capital, national income, and economic growth indicate that changing over to such a system would be well worthwhile.

But in the last analysis, even this question need not be answered. Social security is currently forcing Americans to forgo these enormous returns and to bear the enormous opportunity cost through forced participation in the system. The ultimate issue is whether this is appropriate or whether Americans should be allowed the opportunity to participate in a more productive, fully funded system if they desire and to receive the greater returns of such a system. As will become apparent in succeeding chapters, there are no compensating, offsetting benefits from forcing all Americans into social security's pay-as-you-go system, and indeed there are several additional drawbacks. Consequently, there is no justification for forcing Americans to bear social security's enormous opportunity cost. Americans should be allowed to decide whether they wish to receive the enormous returns available on the investment of the amounts they would otherwise pay in social security taxes. In later chapters, we will discuss how this could be made possible. We should note that Feldstein's critics do not even address the savings issue in terms of opportunity cost.

Labor, Employment, and Economic Efficiency

Social security tends to distort the labor supply, discourage employment, and create economic inefficiencies. These effects have been emphasized over the years by Arthur B. Laffer, professor of business economics at the University of Southern California, and Dr. David Ranson, a Boston-based economist and consultant, although their analysis may differ slightly from that presented here.[16]

The first problem concerns the payroll tax. This tax creates a wedge between what the employer pays and what the employee receives. This

---

[16]The concept of the wedge has been emphasized in the writings of both these economists. For the application of this concept to social security, as well as a discussion of the other problems noted in this section, see Arthur B. Laffer and R. David Ranson, "Some Economic Consequences of the U.S. Social Security System," National Tax Association/Tax Institute of America, Proceedings of the 66th Annual Conference (Toronto, 1973), and Arthur B. Laffer, "Comments on the Social Security System," Conference on Ethics and the Aging Society, 1977.

wedge is equal to the full amount of the social security tax, including both the employer's and the employee's shares, and is borne entirely by the employee. As a result of this wedge, the employee will never be receiving the full value of his work and the full amount paid by his employer, but only this amount minus the wedge or tax. Through this wedge, the tax reduces the compensation of workers and thereby discourages them from working, resulting in a reduced labor supply and reduced employment. The payroll tax is essentially a tax on employment, and here, as elsewhere, the result of taxing something is that there is less of it. With the maximum tax reaching well over $4,000 a year in 1981, and close to $9,000 a year in nominal terms by 1990, the tax is likely to discourage a significant amount of employment.

This would not happen if the employee viewed the payroll tax as a payment for a service he needs or wants, like insurance protection, rather than as a tax. In this case, he would view the tax as part of his wage, like a deduction for mortgage payments or for fringe benefits such as a premium plan or group medical insurance. The employee's tax would in effect be purchasing a service, insurance protection that directly benefits the employee individually and therefore is part of his compensation.

If social security were pure insurance with no welfare elements, the taxpayer would be likely to view his taxes in this way. If the taxpayer were receiving an actuarially fair return in benefits for his tax payments, if there were a direct link between taxes and benefits, with every dollar paid in taxes resulting in a dollar with interest in later benefits, then paying the social security tax would be like putting money in the bank. The employee could expect to receive his taxes back later with interest, and they would therefore be part of his inducement to work.

But social security does not operate this way, and therefore the employee is not likely to view his social security taxes as part of his compensation. All the welfare elements discussed in chapter 2 weaken the link between taxes and benefits so that a dollar of taxes does not bring the worker a dollar of benefits plus interest. Since the worker cannot count on increased tax payments bringing him increased benefits, he will not view his taxes as part of his compensation.

The payroll tax will therefore result in less employment than both workers and employers desire. The wedge prevents employers from hiring as many employees as they would like because it prevents employers from paying directly to employees what they are really worth and from attracting as many workers as they are able and willing to hire at a given hourly expense. The wedge also prevents employees from working as much as they would like at the full wage the employer is willing to pay because they can only receive the after-tax wage for which they are not willing to work as much.

This wedge also causes economic inefficiency and misallocation of resources. Because the wedge prevents labor from receiving its true worth, the labor supply will be below the optimal amount. Workers who can produce $10.61 an hour but only receive $9.39 due to the tax will not supply as much labor as they would if they were paid their full value. Workers who could be producing and taking home $10.61 an hour will instead be consuming leisure time that is only worth $9.40 to $10.60 to them. The economy would thus be using them inefficiently. In the meantime, employers have to make up for the decreased labor supply with increased capital. The resulting mix of capital and labor is a more expensive way of producing the output than the mix of capital and labor that would exist without the tax. This simply means further economic inefficiency and misallocation of resources.

With less employment, economic inefficiency, and misallocation of resources, the result is lower GNP. This loss of GNP adds to the losses from the effect of social security on savings, though it is probably not nearly as great as the losses due to this effect.

Another problem involves the earnings test. As noted earlier, this test reduces benefits for all beneficiaries under the age of seventy-two by $1 for every $2 of wage earnings above a certain limit.

The earnings test again discourages employment by reducing compensation. If social security benefits that the worker is already entitled to receive will be reduced by $1 for every $2 above a certain limit, the worker is in effect receiving only $1 for every $2 worth of his work above that limit. The earnings test thus places a high marginal tax rate of 50 percent on all income earned over the earnings limit until social security benefits are eliminated. In response, workers receiving social security benefits will reduce their work output, and employment will decrease. The elderly in particular may choose to retire earlier, leaving the labor force entirely. This discouraging impact on employment through the earnings test produces the same negative results as the payroll tax.[17]

The third set of social security's negative effects on the labor market results from the loss of savings and capital investment, as discussed earlier. Capital investment increases the productivity of labor and the

[17]It should be noted that those who contend that social security's negative effect on savings is strongly mitigated through induced early retirement and the resulting "retirement effect" on savings are also suggesting that the negative economic effects described here that are due to the earnings test are quite powerful.

demand for it, thereby driving up wages. The reduction in capital investment therefore leads to a loss of higher wages and lower worker productivity. The higher wages might also have induced a greater labor supply, so the loss of capital investment may also mean less employment and less national income.

Capital investment also tends to upgrade jobs and thereby provide more of what are considered good jobs. It does this not only by increasing wages, but also by improving the status of some jobs. For example, capital investment makes steam-shovel operators out of ditch diggers. So the loss of capital investment also means fewer good jobs.

Also, in an economy with persistent unemployment, capital investment will decrease unemployment because of the increased demand for workers necessary for business expansion. Thus, the loss of capital investment caused by social security means a lost opportunity to reduce unemployment.

Welfare vs. Insurance

These negative economic effects of social security are all caused by the conflict between the welfare and insurance objectives of the program. Losses of savings, capital investment, national income, and economic growth are all caused by the operation of the program on a pay-as-you-go basis, which is the result of the pursuit of welfare objectives. As we saw in chapter 2, the program operates on a pay-as-you-go basis because it paid benefits to those in the start-up phase who had paid little into the system themselves, but were all thought needy. But the pursuit of this welfare objective through social security meant that the insurance objective had to be pursued on a pay-as-you-go basis as well, resulting in all the negative economic impacts described above. If retirees in the start-up phase were truly needy, they could have been provided with welfare benefits directly from general revenues, and the negative effects described here would not have occurred. These negative effects are therefore the result of the pursuit of both the incompatible welfare and insurance objectives in the same program.

The negative effects on the labor market resulting from the payroll tax are also due to this conflict in objectives. As discussed earlier, if there were not welfare elements in social security, individuals would view their taxes as a charge for a service they need or want and therefore as part of their compensation. The payroll tax would then not be perceived as reducing compensation and would not discourage employment. It is only because welfare elements are mixed with insurance elements that this problem occurs.

Similarly, as also discussed above, the earnings test itself is one of the welfare elements of the program. It seeks to prevent the payment of benefits to those who are not in need. This would make sense if all social security benefits were welfare benefits, because welfare should not be paid to individuals who are not in need. But social security also includes insurance benefits, and individuals cannot receive insurance benefits that they have paid for unless they meet the earnings test. The result is to discourage employment by all individuals who eventually become entitled to receive these insurance benefits, thus making social security a bad insurance program with unnecessary negative economic effects.

Finally, since the loss of capital investment is caused by the pay-as-you-go system, this problem too is the result of the conflict in objectives.

Conclusion

It is striking that the two primary economic effects of social security are to discourage savings and employment. In the Great Depression, when social security was enacted, such discouragement may have been thought desirable. Keynesian economic theories contended that the depression was caused by inadequate demand, and that saving only decreased this demand, because it was not being offset by increased investment. The social security program, with its pay-as-you-go method of financing, could be seen under these circumstances as a way of decreasing savings and increasing consumption demand. Similarly, it may have been thought that discouraging employment among the elderly and other workers would open up jobs for younger people and ease the unemployment problem.

These policies were probably inappropriate even for the Great Depression.[18] Fifty years later, however, in our modern economy, they

[18]Many have persuasively argued that the Great Depression was caused and continued by mistaken government policies. Murray Rothbard, for example, argues that it was caused by government manipulation of the monetary system in the 1920s. He bases his analysis on the Austrian theory of the business cycle developed by Ludwig Von Mises and Nobel laureate Friedrich Hayek, among others. See Murray N. Rothbard, *America's Great Depression* (Kansas City: Sheed and Ward, 1963); Murray N. Rothbard, *Man, Economy and State* (Los Angeles: Nash, 1970). Nobel laureate Milton Friedman also argues that the depression was caused by government mismanagement of the monetary system, although he bases his analysis on an entirely different theory. See Milton Friedman and Anna Schwartz, *A Monetary History of the United States* (New York: National Bureau of Economic Research, 1963). Jude Wanniski argues that the depression was caused by a number of unwarranted government restrictions on the private economy, the most notable being the oppressive Smoot-Hawley tariff passed in the late 1920s. See Jude Wanniski, *The Way The World Works* (New York: Simon and Schuster, 1978).

are clearly inappropriate. The lost savings exacerbates our capital needs and results in lower national income and economic growth. The losses in GNP caused by the reduction in savings have now grown to $550 billion annually, or approximately $6,600 per family. In addition to this, the program causes losses in employment that result in economic inefficiency and misallocation of resources, all of which depress GNP even further. Discouraging employment among the elderly and other workers does not open up jobs for the young but merely leads to less total employment in the long run.

Because of the tremendous growth of the program in recent years, these negative impacts have now grown to intolerable proportions and will continue to grow as the program gets even larger. But the worst is that these effects are totally unnecessary. They result, as we have seen, simply from the attempt to pursue both welfare and insurance objectives through social security, objectives that are fundamentally incompatible. These negative impacts can therefore be totally eliminated by sensible reforms that will separate the welfare and insurance functions of the present program into two entirely separate programs or sets of institutions.

If the depression was caused and perpetuated by such policies, then the best solution would have been to simply reverse these policies. To the extent that it was necessary for the government to do something to alleviate the problem of dependency it had caused, it probably would have been far preferable to initiate a temporary welfare program for the elderly, with far greater reliance put on private alternatives for provision of old-age support after recovery.

To the extent that social security was structured to help solve the depression, at least some of the economic theories on which it was based are clearly fallacious, and the others have come under increasing question in recent years. Thus, it is commonly accepted among economists that policies to discourage employment among some groups, such as the elderly, do not result in increased employment for other groups, such as the young, but merely result in less total employment in the overall economy in the long run. Furthermore, the whole Keynesian approach has come under increasing question in recent years. Keynesian policies, whether pursued through social security or other means, certainly did not end the depression, and the result of increasing consumption and lowering savings over the years through the pursuit of such policies may well have been merely to lower the overall levels of national income and economic growth.

IV. Social Security and the Individual

"We can't ask support for a plan not at least as good as any American could buy from a private insurance company." So stated the report of the House Subcommittee for Finance in 1935 when Congress was considering passage of the Social Security Act.[1]

But the truth is that young workers entering the social security system today will not do nearly as well in the program as they could participating in private insurance and investment alternatives. If these young persons were allowed to use the money they are expected to pay in social security taxes over the course of their lives to purchase these private alternatives, they would receive far more in return for their money than they would through social security. As will be shown in this chapter, this is true even though those who retired in the early years of the program did in fact receive more through social security than they could have received through private alternatives.

Public vs. Private

The private system of retirement and insurance protection is operated on a fully funded basis. The money paid into the private system is saved and invested and returned to each individual upon retirement. The capital investments made through this system actually increase production and thereby earn the investors a rate of return or interest payment. This increased production is in fact what finances the return or interest payment on these investments. Over the course of a lifetime, this return on investment would accumulate to huge amounts, providing individuals with large estates to support their retirement years. The returns accumulated in these large estates would allow individuals to receive far more in retirement benefits than they paid into the system over the years, all due to the increased production.

Since social security is operated on a pay-as-you-go basis, however, the money taxpayers pay into the system is not saved and invested but is immediately paid out to current recipients. Thus, social security adds nothing to production; it just transfers funds from one part of the population to another. This means that individuals lose the full-interest rate of return they would get on their money if it were invested in private, productive assets. They lose the huge accumulation of assets

---

[1]*Congressional Record,* June 12, 1935, cited in Warren Shore, *Social Security: The Fraud in Your Future* (New York: MacMillan Co., 1975) p. 23.

and large estates, as well as the accompanying higher benefits available under the private, invested system. Since social security does nothing to increase production, each individual can get no more out of the program in benefits than he paid in taxes, unless the government increases the taxes it collects from the next generation of taxpayers to pay his generation increased benefits.

Thus, the essential difference between the private, invested (or fully funded) system and the public, pay-as-you-go system is that the private system increases production and the public system does not. The invested system relies on wealth creation while the pay-as-you-go system relies on mere income redistribution. As a result, the private, invested system can generally pay higher benefits.

Yet empirical comparisons between the private and public systems are tricky because the government can use the power of taxation to make the private system look bad and the public system look good. These appearances, however, are illusory.

The government can, for example, raise taxes on investments in the private sector to such high levels that investors have very little left in returns after taxes. But reduced returns to private investments due to high taxes would not make the private, invested system any the less superior to the public, pay-as-you-go system. Rather, such taxes would merely represent another government barrier preventing individuals from receiving the full benefits of the superior private alternatives. The private investments, even with high taxes, still increase production, but in this situation the government rather than individuals would be receiving most of the benefits of this increased production. Since these increased resources available to the government will either go to provide government services that have been chosen through the political process or to reduce other taxes, individuals in this situation will receive the full benefits of the increased production indirectly, although they may have been better off if they had received these benefits directly in their retirement accounts.[2]

---

[2]Inflation may also reduce the real returns on investments, although over the long run investors should be able to count on a constant real rate of return above inflation. (See footnote 14.) To the extent that inflation does reduce the real returns on investments, it is merely another form of government taxation. Inflation results when the government prints additional money and uses it to purchase goods and services and for other government purposes, such as welfare. Through inflation, therefore, the government in effect appropriates a larger share of national output, as with taxation. This is why inflation is often referred to as the cruelest tax.

Thus, reduced returns to private investments as a result of inflation would mean that the government is again merely siphoning off some of the benefits of the private, invested

36

At the same time that government lowers returns to individuals directly in the private system through high taxes, it can also increase social security taxes on current taxpayers to provide current recipients with high returns in benefits on the taxes they paid into the program. Social security revenues in fact automatically increase over time due to two factors. The first is the rate of growth in real wages. As wages (the tax base) increase over time, the total tax revenues collected from a fixed tax rate on those wages will increase by the rate of growth in those wages. The second factor is the rate of growth in the working population. As this population grows, the total tax collected from a fixed tax rate on the wages of this larger number of people will grow at the rate of growth of this population. In all, total taxes collected will increase by the rate of growth in real wages plus the rate of growth in the working population. The sum of these two rates is usually referred to as the "social security rate of return," in real, inflation-adjusted terms.

In a pay-as-you-go system where all taxes collected are paid out in benefits each year, the real benefits that can be paid are increased annually by this social security real rate of return. An individual who pays taxes into such a pay-as-you-go program all of his life, therefore, will receive back his tax money cumulatively increased by this real rate of return.

Under prevailing empirical conditions, this social security real rate of return is quite low. The rate of growth in real wages over the past three decades has been approximately 1.3 percent or even less.[3] Furthermore, if current trends continue, the population will be declining,[4]

---

system. The total increase in production and wealth from the private system would still be the same, but like direct taxation of investment returns, some of the benefits of this increase would again be provided indirectly through government services or reductions in other taxes. This is not to say that this inflation/taxation process is legitimate or that individuals on net are not made worse off by all the negative effects of inflation. It is merely to note that reduced real returns to private investments due to inflation do not make the private system any the less superior to social security.

[3]The rate of growth in real wages from 1952 to 1975 was 1.3 percent. Martin Feldstein, "Facing the Social Security Crisis," Harvard Institute of Economic Research, Discussion Paper no. 492, July 2, 1976. From 1952 to 1977, this average was 1.37 percent, based on data from the Social Security Administration. Since then, real wage growth has been lower, and even negative in some years.

[4]The fertility rate for 1980 was 1.84. Social Security Board of Trustees, *1981 Annual Report of the Board of Trustees of the Old-Age and Survivors Insurance and Disability Insurance Trust Funds* (Washington, D.C., April 1, 1982), p.35. To maintain a constant population, the fertility rate must be 2.1. The 1980 fertility rate was at a level which had been basically maintained for 5 years, after a persistent decline in fertility rates for the prior 200 years.

which could conceivably overwhelm the effects from the increase in real wages, making the overall social security rate of return negative. Even if recent fertility trends did turn around, the strength of these trends and the strong social forces behind them make it unlikely that population would grow enough in the foreseeable future to add significantly to the social security rate of return.

In fact, social security is likely to experience the effects of a declining population in the near future even if such a decline does not actually occur. During the fifteen-year "baby boom" immediately following World War II fertility rates increased rapidly. Since then, however, fertility rates have declined dramatically, reaching the lowest levels in the nation's history.[5] This baby bust, following so soon after the baby boom, creates the effects of a declining population for social security. When the baby boom generation begins to retire, with the baby bust generation working, the number of workers relative to the number of retirees will fall, as in a declining population. If recent fertility trends continue, the number of beneficiaries per one hundred workers will increase from thirty-one today to sixty-three in 2025.[6] This decline in the working population relative to the retired population means that at fixed tax rates, taxes will be insufficient to meet escalating benefit obligations. Indeed, if fertility trends continue, tax rates will have to double by 2025 to maintain benefits at expected levels. This strongly suggests that the impact on social security from these demographic factors will be to make the social security real rate of return negative.

Compared to these very low or negative returns under social security for the foreseeable future, the before-tax, real rate of return on private capital investments is 12 to 13 percent.[7] Even in the best of times, historical conditions indicate that the social security real rate of return will never be more than 3 to 4 percent.

For a more detailed discussion of this issue see Ferrara, *Social Security: The Inherent Contradiction*, chap. 5.

[5]The lowest fertility rate in the nation's history was 1.74 in 1976, and the rate has basically remained close to this number since then, after a persistent drop over the prior 200 years, as discussed in footnote 4. See Ferrara, *Social Security: The Inherent Contradiction*, chap. 5.

[6]Social Security Board of Trustees, *1982 Annual Report of the Board of Trustees of the Federal Old-Age and Survivors Insurance and Disability Insurance Trust Funds* (Washington, D.C., April 1, 1982). These provisions were made under the alternative III set of assumptions in the report which, although designated as the pessimistic set of assumptions, assumed that the fertility rate would remain basically the same as it is today.

[7]See footnote 13.

Regardless of the level of this social security rate of return, or any higher pay-as-you-go returns paid from further tax increases,[8] this return is entirely different from the returns generated by the private, invested system. Private returns come from increased production generated by the private, invested system itself. They are, therefore, self-financing and do not constitute a burden to anyone. Any return paid through a public, pay-as-you-go system, however, is merely generated by increased taxes. There is no increased production to pay for it, and it therefore constitutes a burden on current workers. It is only the result of redistribution, and thus retirees are being made better off only by making workers worse off. Regardless of the level of this return, individuals under the pay-as-you-go system still lose the full rate of return, or amount of newly created wealth, resulting from the private, invested system.

As an example, assume that the returns through both the pay-as-you-go and the invested, fully funded systems were the same, say 2 percent. In the pay-as-you-go system, the return would be paid by charging the current working generation sufficiently more in taxes than the current retired generation paid when it was working to finance this 2 percent. But in the invested system this 2 percent return would be paid by the increased production or wealth created by the system's investments. The current working generation could then keep the additional amounts it would have paid in taxes under the pay-as-you-go system. As long as this generation continued to save and invest for its retirement the increased wealth generated by its retirement investments, it would be able to receive the same benefits as it would have received under the pay-as-you-go system, without saving and investing the additional amounts it would have otherwise had to pay into the pay-as-you-go system. If this generation did save and invest these additional amounts for its own retirement as well, its retirement benefits would be increased by both these additional amounts and the additional accumulated returns they would generate through increased production. These advantages of the private, invested system over the public, pay-as-you-go system are all due to the injection of newly created wealth into the system each year, wealth that is created by the

---

[8]There is, of course, a limit to such further increases. They cannot go on forever for both political and economic reasons. We appear to be approaching that limit already, and it is therefore highly unlikely that there will be sufficient further tax increases in future years to pay individuals a significant rate of return beyond the social security rate of return. See Ferrara, *Social Security: The Inherent Contradiction,* chap. 4.

system itself and that is not available to the pay-as-you-go system.[9]

Thus, the private, invested system remains monetarily superior to the public, pay-as-you-go system, even when part of the returns of the invested system are taxed away and payroll taxes are increased to raise the return under the pay-as-you-go system. This is so even though in the past many individuals received much higher returns and benefits under social security than they could have received under private, invested alternatives. These past high returns were due to the effects of the start-up phase of the program, and these returns are now disappearing as the program enters the mature phase. As we have noted, in the start-up phase of a pay-as-you-go program, the first working generation is paying taxes, but since these taxes are not saved and invested, they can be used to pay full benefits to current retirees in the first retired generation who have paid little or nothing in past taxes themselves. The result is that these early retirees receive very high returns on whatever they have paid into the program. But over time these returns will fall as more and more workers retire, having paid full taxes for most of their working lives. Eventually, as the program enters the mature stage, retirees (generally, the second retired generation) will have paid a lifetime of full taxes, and they can therefore receive, without further tax increases, only the social security rate of return resulting from increasing wages and population. As we have seen, this return will be very low, if not negative, in future years.

America's social security system is just now entering the mature phase; so future generations of retirees will receive the low, below-market returns of the mature pay-as-you-go system, which translates into lower benefits than would be received through private, invested alternatives. The developing inferiority of social security to private, invested alternatives is particularly clear in the case of young workers entering the work force today, as we shall see below.

It should be emphasized that even the transitory above-market returns in the start-up phase of a pay-as-you-go system are not the result of increased production but of increased taxation on the first generation of workers. These returns, therefore, simply result from making this first generation of workers worse off through the appropriation and redistribution of a substantial portion of their incomes. As we have noted, to the extent that these returns were above market rates, they in fact constituted a simple welfare subsidy paid to all in the first

---

[9]See Appendix.

generation of retirees, regardless of need. The indiscriminate payment of such welfare subsidies has to be considered an unconscionable waste of taxpayers' scarce resources. Moreover, the high returns of the start-up phase are payable only at the cost of locking all future generations into the inferior, mature phase of the program.

This theoretical discussion thus leads to the conclusion that the private, invested system can pay substantially higher benefits than the public, pay-as-you-go system. An empirical comparison between these two systems will strongly support this conclusion.

An Empirical Comparison

Our comparison focuses on three hypothetical workers who enter the work force in 1980.[10] One is twenty-four and earns a salary equal to the maximum taxable income all of his life, an earnings history typical of professional employees. The second is twenty-two and earns the average salary in social security-covered employment all of his life, a salary somewhat less than that earned by the typical male head of household or unionized blue-collar worker. The third is eighteen and earns the rough equivalent of the minimum wage all of his life, an earnings history of an unusually poor worker.

Based on assumptions provided by the Social Security Board of Trustees, we have projected the annual amounts under the current social security system that each of these individuals would pay in social security taxes (OASDHI), including both the employer and employee shares of the tax, over the course of his working years. We have then deducted from these annual totals sufficient amounts to purchase for each worker private life and disability insurance policies that would provide coverage equivalent to that provided by social security's survivors' and disability insurance programs. The benefits paid by these private policies are in fact monetarily superior to those paid by social security, as we shall see. After deducting the amounts for these policies, we next assume that the remainder of the annual social security tax amounts are saved and invested for each worker through his own private retirement trust fund. Finally, we have calculated the amount of retirement benefits that could be paid to each worker by such a trust fund. These are compared below to the retirement benefits that would be paid to each worker by social security, including the old-age hospital insurance benefits.

[10]For a more detailed discussion of the underlying elements of this comparison and the results, see Ferrara, *Social Security: The Inherent Contradiction*, chap. 4.

The Board of Trustees' assumptions underlying these projections came from their 1978 Annual Report.[11] Each year, the trustees publish in their annual report projections of the program's future performance based on three alternative sets of assumptions—Alternative I, the optimistic set; Alternative II, the intermediate set; and Alternative III, the pessimistic set. (In the 1981 and 1982 Annual Reports, the trustees divided the intermediate set into an optimistic intermediate set, Alternative IIA, and pessimistic intermediate set, Alternative IIB, which basically differed in their assumptions relating to the short-run performance of the economy.) In 1978, as in most years, Alternative III was actually the most realistic set of assumptions. Under this alternative, virtually all of the economic and social factors considered were assumed to simply continue the trends established in recent years. Under Alternative II, virtually every one of these factors was assumed to reverse their recent trends and move in a favorable direction. Under Alternative I, virtually every factor was assumed not only to reverse recent trends, but to move in a favorable direction by an unrealistically wide margin.[12] We will discuss the projections made under Alternative II, although projections under all these alternatives can be found in the tables.

The remaining major assumption of the study involved the real rate of return that could be earned by the private system's investments. According to Professor Feldstein, a real rate of return of 8 percent is quite possible and 5.5 percent is conservative. Feldstein writes:

> Over the past twenty-five years, the real annual yield (after adjusting for inflation) was 8% for common stock and 3% for corporate bonds. A conservative portfolio with half of each would have yielded 5.5%.[13]

In fact, if half of the annual payments into our system of private trust funds was invested each year in common stocks with an 8 percent real return and half was invested each year in corporate bonds with a 3 percent real return, and the 8 percent return to common stocks was reinvested each year in common stocks and the 3 percent return on corporate bonds was reinvested each year in corporate bonds, the average yield on the fund after forty-one years would be 6.3 percent, not 5.5 percent.

[11]Board of Trustees, *1978 Annual Report of the Board of Trustees of the Federal Old-Age and Survivors Insurance and Disability Insurance Trust Funds*, May 15, 1978.

[12]For a more detailed discussion of the assumptions underlying these three alternatives, see Ferrara, *Social Security: The Inherent Contradiction*, chap. 5.

[13]Martin Feldstein, "Facing the Social Security Crisis," *Harvard Institute of Economic Research*, Discussion Paper no. 492, July 1976, p. 5.

The record more than supports Feldstein's position. From 1945 to 1976, the average real rate of return earned on common stocks listed on the New York Stock Exchange was 7.5 percent. From 1945 to 1972, the return was 9.6 percent, and from 1945 to 1965, 12 percent. If we change the basic date of reference, we find that from 1926 to 1976, a fifty-year period including the Great Depression, the real rate of return on common stocks was 6.9 percent. From 1926 to 1972, this return was exactly 8 percent, and from 1926 to 1965, 9 percent. The return from 1933 to 1976 was 8 percent, from 1933 to 1972—9.4 percent, and from 1933 to 1965—10.9 percent. These average returns include those stocks where the company went bankrupt during the year, thus creating a sharply negative rate of return for that particular stock for that year.[14]

Yet these are only the after-tax returns that would be earned by private investments, the returns left after considerable taxes on these investments had been paid through the corporate income tax and other tax levies.[15] But as our theoretical discussion above indicates, a truly fair comparison between social security and private, invested alternatives would require us to compare the real, *before-tax* returns under the private system with the returns under social security. These before-tax returns represent the full benefits available under the invested system, even if some of them are used through taxation to provide government services. Since social security provides no revenue for these non-social security government expenditures, the full benefits the invested system can pay without providing any such revenues should be considered as well.

According to Feldstein and others, the full real before-tax rate of return on capital investments is conservatively estimated at 12 to 13 percent, as we haved noted.[16] In the final chapter we will propose a

---

[14]Roger G. Ibbotson and Rex A. Sinquefeld, *Stocks, Bonds, Bills and Inflation: The Past (1926–1976) and The Future (1977–2000)* (Chicago: Financial Analysts Research Foundation, 1977).

[15]Although in many circumstances an individual may still have to pay some additional income taxes on this return, tax exemptions available today through Individual Retirement Accounts (IRAs), Keogh plans, and similar types of tax-preferred pension plans would largely eliminate this taxation. We can therefore take this return as the real, after-tax return available on investments that can be made through a private retirement fund.

[16]Martin Feldstein, "National Saving in the United States," *Harvard Institute of Economic Research*, Discussion Paper no. 506, October 1976; Martin Feldstein, "Toward a Reform of Social Security," *Public Interest*, Summer 1975, pp. 75–95; Martin Feldstein, "The Optional Financing of Social Security," *Harvard Institute of Economic Research*, Discussion Paper no. 338, 1974; Alicia H. Munnell, *The Future of Social Security* (Washington, D.C.: The Brookings Institution, 1977), p. 128.

system of tax exemptions for investments made through individual retirement and insurance accounts as an alternative to social security. This system of tax exemptions would allow individuals to receive this full real before-tax rate of return on the capital investments made through these accounts.

We have made our comparison between social security and private, invested alternatives under eleven different assumed real rates of return on the private investments, ranging from 3.0 percent to 8.0 percent. We will discuss here the results assuming a 6.0 percent real rate of return. These results can be taken as the benefits available under the private, invested system based only on after-tax returns, or, considering the data discussed above and the recommended enactment of the proposed new tax exemption system discussed in chapter 10, as a very conservative estimate of the benefits available based on before-tax returns.

It should be emphasized that both the social security and the private alternative benefits presented in this comparison were calculated in constant 1980 dollars. These benefits will therefore not be depreciated by inflation over the years. The actual nominal dollar amounts the worker would receive under both systems would be increased by the rate of inflation between now and the time the worker receives them. The benefits paid by the private system would thereafter be increased each year to compensate for inflation, as would the benefits paid by social security.[17]

The projections of the amounts individuals would have in their retirement trust funds at age sixty-five, and the amounts these funds could pay each year in retirement benefits, are shown in tables 8–16. The retirement fund and benefit amounts are shown for each of the different assumed real rates of return. The projections for maximum, average,

---

[17]This is especially important because government officials have heavily emphasized the fact that social security benefits are indexed to rise with the rate of inflation and have contended that this inflation-proof feature of the program cannot be matched by private alternatives. This is simply not true. As prices increase with inflation, the prices charged for the goods and services produced by the investments in the private, invested system will also increase, on average, at the same rate. As a result, the returns on these investments will tend to increase with inflation, and a constant real rate of return after inflation will be maintained. Similarly, the value of the assets that individuals hold in their invested retirement accounts will also increase, on average, at the rate of inflation, maintaining the real value of these assets. This is the process that maintained the real rates of return that we noted in the text for one simple pattern of investments—a broad-based holding of stocks on the New York Stock Exchange. The ability of the private invested system to pay these real rates of return, as maintained through this process, means that this system can provide individuals with a constant, real level of benefits, adjusted annually for inflation.

and low-income workers are shown three times, once for each of the three alternative sets of assumptions discussed above.

The *perpetual annuity* column shows the amounts that could be paid each year out of interest on the fund alone, leaving the fund intact to be passed on to the worker's children or other heirs. The *life annuity for a single worker* column shows the amounts that could be paid each year for the life of the worker after age sixty-five, completely using up the fund. The *life annuity for a couple* column shows the amounts that could be paid, completely using up the fund, while both spouses are alive and after one spouse dies. At the bottom of each table, we also show the amount that social security would pay a single worker, with the earnings noted, and the amount that social security would pay such a worker with a spouse, while both were alive, and after one died.

In parentheses, next to each benefit amount, is the replacement ratio that this benefit amount represents. The replacement ratio is the annual benefit amount as a percentage of the individual's income during his last year of work. A replacement ratio of 65 percent to 75 percent of pretax income is sufficient to maintain a retiree's standard of living because of the reduced expenses of retirement.

Under our selected assumptions, our maximum income worker (table 11) would retire at age sixty-five with a retirement trust fund of $995,320 in constant 1980 dollars, or approximately $1 million. This fund could pay the worker $59,719 in constant 1980 dollars each year out of the interest alone. This would allow the worker and his spouse to enjoy this annual income until both died and still leave the million-dollar fund to their children. Alternatively, the worker could use the fund to purchase an annuity that would pay $96,939 annually in constant 1980 dollars until he or his spouse died, and $64,626 until the surviving spouse died.

Social security would pay this worker $23,326 each year in constant 1980 dollars until he or his spouse died, and $15,551 until the surviving spouse died. In addition, social security would provide hospital insurance coverage worth $1,000 per year for each spouse while alive. Social security, of course, never leaves the worker with a trust fund to pass on to his children. Thus the private system could pay this worker about four times what social security would pay, or, alternatively, it could pay well over twice what social security would pay while still allowing the worker to leave approximately $1 million to his children. Furthermore, if both the worker and his spouse worked as professionals and both earned the maximum taxable amount, an increasingly common phenomenon, the trust fund amount and benefits paid under the private system would double. Social security benefits, however, would remain the same except that the annual benefit paid while both spouses were alive would increase by only one third, to $31,102.

Similarly, the worker earning an average salary all of his life (table 12) would retire at age sixty-five with a trust fund of $469,662 in constant 1980 dollars. This fund could pay the worker and his spouse $28,180 per year in constant 1980 dollars out of the interest alone. Again, the worker and his spouse could enjoy this annual income until both had died, and then still leave the half-million-dollar fund to their children. Alternatively, they could purchase an annuity with the fund that would pay $45,743 annually in constant 1980 dollars while both were alive and $30,495 until the survivor died. Social security would pay this worker $15,408 per year in constant 1980 dollars with both spouses alive and $10,272 with only one alive, along with the $1,000 per year per spouse in hospital insurance coverage. Thus the private system would pay this worker about three times what social security would pay, or alternatively, it would pay twice what social security would pay while still allowing the average worker to leave a half million to his children. In addition, if both spouses worked and earned average salaries, the private benefits would again double while social security benefits would remain the same, except that the annual benefit paid while both spouses were alive would increase by one third, to $20,544.

As we have noted, the social security program contains many welfare elements that operate to pay poor workers relatively more in benefits compared to their past taxes than higher-income workers. Yet even poor workers would do substantially better under the private alternative system than under social security. Based again on our selected assumptions, our poor workers (table 13) would retire at age sixty-five with a trust fund of $287,798 in constant 1980 dollars, well over one-quarter million. This fund could pay the worker and his spouse $17,268 annually in constant 1980 dollars until both died, while still allowing them to leave the entire one-quarter-million-dollar fund to their children. Alternatively, they could purchase an annuity paying $28,030 per year in 1980 dollars with both alive and $18,687 until the survivor died. Social security would pay $10,080 per year in 1980 dollars with both alive and $6,720 until the survivor died, along with the $1,000 per spouse each year in hospital insurance coverage. Thus the private system would pay this poor worker almost three times what social security would pay or, alternatively, it could pay 50 percent more than social security would pay, and allow the poor worker to leave one-quarter million to his children. Once again, if both spouses worked

46

and earned the same low salaries, the private benefits would double, while social security benefits would remain the same except for a one-third increase in the annual benefit with both spouses alive, to $13,440.[18]

In addition to these advantages, the private alternative system also maintained similar advantages in the area of life (survivors') and disability insurance. In both of these areas, the private system was able to pay to all individuals during their earlier working years—their twenties, thirties, and early forties—the maximum benefits available under social security. But social security would pay such maximum benefits only to individuals with large families, including a dependent spouse and a number of dependent minor children. In addition, during the later working years when workers are most likely to die or become disabled—their late forties, fifties, and early sixties—the private system could pay more than the social security maximum. These are also the years when workers are less likely to have enough dependent minor children to receive the maximum under social security. Finally, if a worker's spouse also works and earns an equivalent wage, the benefits under the private system would roughly double while the benefits under social security would remain approximately the same.[19]

[18]It is true that the investments of some private pension funds and other retirement vehicles have received relatively low real rates of return in the past few years. This performance is due to three factors. First, these investments are still heavily taxed, particularly through the corporate income tax, and they are therefore not allowed to receive the full, real before-tax rate of return we have noted.

Second, the sudden jump in inflation in recent years caught many businessmen and investors by surprise. This increase has cut the profits of many businesses and resulted in lower real rates of return on capital investments. But the most fundamental economic theory tells us that this is a transitory phenomenon and that historical real rates of return will be reestablished as businesses and investors adjust to inflationary trends. (See footnote 16.)

The third reason for the weak performance of many private retirement investments in recent years is that these investments are heavily regulated. These regulations are too stringent and overly protective, and as a result, they prevent pension investors from making the lucrative yet sufficiently safe investments that they could otherwise make.

None of these three factors suggests that the private, alternative system is any the less superior to social security than we have indicated. The full benefits of the private system are still represented by the full, real before-tax return on capital investments of 12–13 percent, which is the degree to which the private system increases production above what social security does. If the government is taking certain actions that prevent individuals from receiving these benefits and that result in appropriation of these benefits by the government itself, the benefits of the private system are not therefore any less. These government actions must be changed as well so that individuals can receive the full private benefits they ought to receive.

[19]For a more detailed discussion of the superiority of the private system in these areas of survivors' and disability insurance, see Ferrara, *Social Security: The Inherent Contradiction,* chap. 4.

The private system thus appears to be remarkably superior to social security in simple monetary terms for workers of all income classes. Though this advantage is relatively less in absolute terms for low-income workers, it is probably more important to these workers because it will provide them with the means to buy more basic necessities and to attain a decent standard of living. Moreover, these poor workers will have earned these higher living standards solely through their own work, skill, and effort, rather than through government handouts. The private system will also enable low-income workers to enjoy these benefits while still leaving them with large trust funds, which they can use to help their children and grandchildren break out of the cycle of poverty and attain even higher standards of living. And at the same time that many low-income workers will be receiving these advantages of the private system, the welfare elements of the current social security program that favor low-income workers could be continued in a separate, simple welfare program for those still unable to attain decent living standards.

There are also a number of important ways in which the private system is qualitatively superior to social security. First, in the private system each individual could tailor his own package of insurance and investment purchases to suit his own needs and preferences. Social security, in contrast, forces everyone to accept one plan of insurance protection with one set of benefit provisions. But there is no one plan that can match the widely varying needs and preferences of everyone. The result is that under social security many individuals are forced to purchase a plan of insurance protection that is poorly suited to their individual circumstances. For example, social security forces single workers to pay for survivors' insurance even though they have no family members who could ever become eligible for survivors' benefits. Under the private system, individuals would not be forced to purchase insurance that could never pay them anything.

Secondly, only social security benefits are subject to numerous conditions that can result in lower payments. For example, under social security a surviving wife with children must remain unmarried to receive her full survivors' benefits. Under the private system, she would be free to get married if she chooses. Under social security, if she works and earns over a certain amount, her benefits will be cut under the earnings test. Under the private system, her benefits would remain the same no matter how much she earned.

Finally, under the private system each individual would actually retain ownership over the amounts he paid into the system. He would therefore have the right to retain control over the assets accumulated in his private, individual retirement account. He could then use these assets to take advantage of special business opportunities and investments. Even if the worker could not actually dip into such accounts or other insurance proceeds for consumption until he became a beneficiary, he could still use his funds to make gifts or provide other special support to children or grandchildren, to buy a home or make other special purchases, or to accelerate benefit payments for an emergency or other reason. Thus, in contrast to social security, individuals would be able to use their accumulated assets and future benefit entitlements in ways that most benefit them.

Conclusion

Social security is enormously inferior to private alternatives, both monetarily and qualitatively, for young workers entering the program today. And now that the program has reached the mature stage, social security will remain inferior for all future generations. The inferiority of the program in the mature stage is in fact so great that social security has now become intolerably unfair to young workers and to all workers who will enter the work force in the future. Reform is therefore now absolutely necessary to allow these workers to receive the superior benefits of the private alternatives.

The problems we have discussed in this chapter are again due to the conflict between the welfare and insurance goals of the program. As we have shown, the chief reason that social security is inferior to private alternatives is that the program is operated on a pay-as-you-go basis rather than on an invested basis. But as we have noted, the program is operated in this way solely because welfare objectives are pursued along with insurance objectives. It was again the payment of unearned and unpaid-for benefits to those who were thought to be in need in the early years of the program that led to its operation on a pay-as-you-go basis. Thus, the pursuit of these welfare objectives through the program has led to the problems in the program's pursuit of insurance objectives that we have noted in this chapter.[20]

These problems can all be solved, however, by separating the welfare functions of the program from insurance functions, and then allowing today's young workers out of the program to use the money they would have paid in social security taxes to invest in private alternatives. This

---

[20]The qualitative shortcomings of social security that we have noted are also due to the conflict between the welfare and insurance objectives of the program. Ibid.

would have to be accomplished while still meeting currently accrued benefit obligations and phasing out the unfunded liability of the program. A proposal to accomplish this will be presented in chapter 10.

Appendix

The points made in this paragraph might be further illustrated by diagram A. Unshaded portions of the bars represent the amount in taxes or payments paid each of four years by a single generation under both the pay-as-you-go and invested, fully-funded systems, assuming a 2 percent real rate of return for each. Starting out at 100 units a year, under the pay-as-you-go system the amount paid must increase by 2 percent each year to finance the system's benefits. Under the invested system, however, these amounts need not be paid since the benefits of retirees are fully financed out of their own investments. But an equivalent additional amount is invested each year under this system due to the accumulation and reinvestment of the 2 percent real rate of return generated each year by the system's investments. This is the portion of each bar shaded by lines under the invested or fully funded system in the diagram. Thus the same benefits can ultimately be paid by the invested system without the use of the amounts that would otherwise have had to be paid into the pay-as-you-go system each year. If these amounts are also added to the invested system, the amount accumulated each year would grow faster, and eventually higher benefits could be paid. These additional amounts are shown as the portion of each bar shaded by dots. Either these spotted portions or the lined portions of each bar could be taken as a measure of the additional wealth produced by the invested system, which results because the invested system increases production cumulatively by, in this case, 2 percent annually, while the pay-as-you-go system does nothing to increase production. Therefore, it is a measure of the monetary superiority of the invested system even when the putative rate of return under each system is the same. The portion of each bar shaded by circles is the amount accumulated from the past, along with its investment returns, that would be added to the invested system each year if the amounts otherwise required by the pay-as-you-go system were also added to the invested system. This does not include the amount that would have been required by the pay-as-you-go system in that year, which is the portion shaded by dots.

DIAGRAM A

PAY-AS-YOU-GO SYSTEM

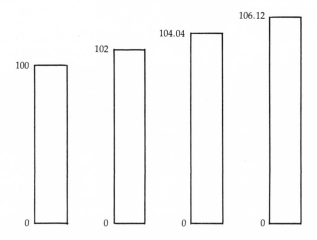

INVESTED OR FULLY-FUNDED SYSTEM

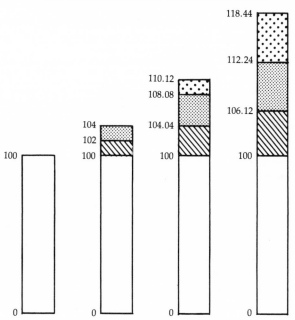

V. Social Security and Bankruptcy

In 1977 Congress enacted one of the largest tax increases in U.S. history. Its purpose was to save the social security system from bankruptcy. Under the new law, social security payroll tax rates will increase steadily through 1990. Yet according to official projections of the Social Security Administration, even this massive tax increase will not be sufficient to prevent future threats of bankruptcy.

Bankruptcy is defined here as the inability of the program to fulfill all the benefit promises it is currently making to future beneficiaries. These promises are made to today's taxpayers to convince them to continue paying their taxes. Today's workers are being lulled into making their future plans based on such promises. The inability of the program to fulfill these promises would, therefore, be a major social, economic, moral, and political problem. And, despite the attempt by many to downplay the significance of this potentially enormous problem, the threat of bankruptcy for the social security system remains quite real.

The Maturity of the Program

This problem of potential bankruptcy is again due to the developing maturity of social security's pay-as-you-go system. When a pay-as-you-go system is begun, a full generation of taxpayers begins to pay taxes, but there are then no beneficiaries entitled to benefits based on past tax payments. In the start-up phase, the program therefore appears to be running up huge surpluses. There is no concern over meeting the obligations of the program because the program has no obligations.

In an invested system, the initial funds paid into the program would have to be saved and invested to finance the future benefits of current workers. But in a pay-as-you-go system, the taxes of the next generation of workers will pay for the benefits of current workers so the initial tax receipts are not invested.

Thus, in the initial start-up phase of a pay-as-you-go system, Congress can use whatever tax receipts are generated to pass out free, windfall benefits to the first generation of retirees. With the program generating huge unclaimed surpluses, the system appears to have eminent financial soundness. Current recipients are experiencing a windfall, current taxpayers are assured that their old age is secure, and current politicians are hailed as great humanitarians.

As the system enters the mature stage, however, the retiring generation will have paid taxes for an entire lifetime and will thereby have built up enormous benefit claims. At this point, there are no more unclaimed surpluses and no more free benefits to pass out. The problem now becomes whether taxes from today's workers will be sufficient to pay the liabilities owed to those now retiring. The task of Congress is now to increase taxes on the current generation of workers until enough funds are raised to finance the program's obligations. The question is whether Congress will be as good at this task as it was in handing out free benefits and whether politicians will still be considered great humanitarians.

It is thus only in the mature stage that bankruptcy becomes a real threat. It is only in the mature stage that the program will have accrued a full complement of liabilities—the enormous obligation of providing support for an entire generation of retired Americans. A potential problem now develops because the program has accumulated no assets to aid in the payment of these liabilities. Such payment depends solely on the maintenance of sufficient current tax revenues to meet the accrued benefit obligations.

At this point, the program becomes particularly vulnerable to any social or economic developments that might cause increases in benefit payments or declines in tax receipts, thereby upsetting the delicate balance between taxes and benefits in a pay-as-you-go system. Such developments could in fact now be disastrous for the program if taxpayers are unwilling to make up the difference through increased taxes.

The previous thirty to forty years of operation of America's social security system have proved nothing about the stability and viability of a pay-as-you-go system because most of that time has been the initial start-up phase. It is just in recent years that the emphasis has turned from paying out surplus benefits to raising taxes to meet huge obligations. But already there are social and economic developments threatening the fragile balance of social security's pay-as-you-go system. These developments have created both a short-term and a long-term financing problem.

Economic Effects and the Short-Term Problem

One of the factors to which a mature pay-as-you-go system is particularly vulnerable is the short-term performance of the economy. Since the system relies on the payroll tax for funding, an increase in unemployment results in fewer workers paying taxes and, therefore, a decline in expected revenues. Similarly, a decline in the rate of growth in wages or in the rate of growth in employment also means a decline in expected social security payroll tax revenues. A recession has all three of these effects and consequently recessions can have, and have had, devastating effects on the solvency of social security.

In addition, since social security benefits are indexed to rise automatically with inflation, an increase in inflation causes an increase in total social security expenditures. Rapidly accelerating inflation alone, therefore, can also have devastating effects on social security financing arrangements. But when persistently high inflation is combined with periodic sharp recessions, creating stagflation, as has been the case in the American economy in recent years, the effect is particularly devastating. Benefit expenditures will be rising above expected levels at the same time that tax revenues are falling below expected levels. This problem is exacerbated even further when stagflation causes inflation to rise faster than wages. In such an economic climate, benefits in a mature pay-as-you-go system will naturally tend to outrace taxes. Just such a combination of economic events is once again causing serious financing problems for social security.[1] The unemployment and poor wage growth during the 1979–80 recession caused social security tax revenues to decline sharply from expected levels at the same time that record inflation was causing benefits to increase dramatically. The even sharper 1981–82 recession has caused tax receipts to fall off even more dramatically from expected levels. The 1982 annual reports of the Board of Trustees for the Social Security trust funds projected that this combination of inflation and recession would cause the combined OASDI portion of the program to run short of funds sometime in 1983.[2] If a

[1]Such a combination of economic factors also caused the social security financing problem in the mid-1970s. The recession in the early 1970s caused unemployment to rise sharply while real wages fell. At the same time, inflation continued, increasing benefits; as a result, tax revenues fell sharply below benefit levels. While taxes exceeded benefits for the OASDI program in 1974 by $0.4 billion, this changed to a $2.7 billion deficit in 1975, growing to $4.1 billion in 1976 and $5.9 billion in 1977. See Social Security Board of Trustees, *1980 Annual Report of the Board of Trustees of the Federal Old-Age and Survivors Insurance and Disability Insurance Trust Funds* (Washington, D.C., June 17, 1980). Because real wages had not grown as fast during the recession as expected, wages were left on a permanently lower growth path incapable of generating the tax revenues necessary to finance projected benefits. The result was steadily increasing deficits exacerbated by continued sluggish wage growth. The trust funds were projected to be exhausted by the end of the decade, leaving social security unable to meet its benefit promises. Only the massive tax increase in 1977 saved the system from bankruptcy.

[2]Social Security Board of Trustees, *1982 Annual Report of the Board of Trustees of the Federal Old-Age and Survivors Insurance and Disability Insurance Trust Funds* (Washington, D.C., April 1, 1982).

55

portion of HI taxes are used to pay OASDI benefits, the report projects that the entire OASDI program is likely to be unable to pay benefits sometime in 1984.[3]

All this only two years after the 1978 annual report of the Board of Trustees stated, concerning the 1977 tax increases:

> The Social Security Amendments of 1977, enacted on December 20, 1977, restore the financial soundness of the cash benefit program throughout the remainder of this century and into the early years of the next one.[4]

It is incredible that even with these recent massive tax increases, a major financing problem has again developed in the program in the next few years, necessitating further tax increases or benefit reductions.

The problem of the vulnerability of the program to short-term economic trends is exacerbated by the fact that even tax increases may not be able to solve the resulting financing problems. Tax increases themselves could create economic conditions that would lead to declines in tax revenues, rather than increases, or to smaller increases than expected. As the wedge between what the employer pays and what the employee receives continues to grow with tax increases, employment will be discouraged more and more. As employment falls, so do tax revenues. This decline in employment could lead to declines in consumer demand that, under Keynesian assumptions, could cause further unemployment and declines in tax revenues. Higher taxes are also likely to lead to further reductions in savings and capital investment, which would lead to even slower wage growth and lower total employment, depressing total tax revenues even further. It is conceivable that we could reach

---

[3]The 1982 Annual Reports projected the actuarial status of the program under four different assumptions—optimistic (Alternative I), optimistic intermediate (Alternative IIA), pessimistic intermediate (Alternative IIB), and pessimistic (Alternative III). The chief difference between Alternatives IIA and IIB is that the former assumes a quick, sharp recovery from the early 1982 recession and the latter predicts a slower and weaker one. Based on current trends, Alternative IIB, or even Alternative III, appear to be the most realistic assumptions, with the recession recovery in particular behaving much more as assumed under these alternatives than under the other two. Under either Alternative IIB or Alternative III, the entire OASDI program would fall short of revenues in 1984 if HI taxes were used to tide over the OASDI portion of the program in 1983. Even under Alternative IIA, the program is left with no margin for error. If the economy performs less well than assumed by only the slightest margin, the entire program will still run short of funds. Ibid.

[4]Social Security Board of Trustees, *1978 Annual Report of the Board of Trustees of the Federal Old-Age and Survivors Insurance and Disability Insurance Trust Funds* (Washington, D.C., May 15, 1978), p. 3.

56

a point where the economy simply would not support the burden of social security benefit promises and their accompanying tax burdens under the pay-as-you-go framework.

Demographic Effects and the Long-Term Problem

For a mature pay-as-you-go system, population changes are critically important. Since current retirees are entirely dependent on the taxes paid by today's workers, anything which increases the number of retirees or decreases the number of workers will make financing more difficult and require higher tax rates. The United States has undergone a series of population changes in recent years that will tend to both increase the number of retirees and decrease the number of workers in the future.[5]

As noted in chapter 4, fertility rates in the past two decades have fallen to their lowest levels in U.S. history. This sharp decline began immediately after the baby boom of the 1950s, which means that the future resulting decline in the number of workers relative to retirees will be accentuated even further. The Social Security Board of Trustees projects that if current demographic trends continue,[6] by the time young people entering the work force today retire, there could be as many as 63 beneficiaries for every 100 workers compared with 31 per 100 today. This 100 percent increase suggests that taxes will only be sufficient to finance 50 percent of the expected benefits at that time,

[5]For a more detailed discussion of these population changes, see Ferrara, *Social Security: The Inherent Contradiction*, chap. 5.

[6]Social Security Board of Trustees, *1982 Annual Report of the Board of Trustees of the Federal Old-Age and Survivors Insurance and Disability Insurance Trust Funds*, (Washington, D.C., April 1, 1982). These projections were made under the Alternative III set of assumptions in the report which, although designated as the pessimistic set of assumptions, assumed that fertility trends will continue to follow the pattern established in recent years. Although the fertility rate has been volatile since World War II, it appears that current fertility trends are here to stay for the foreseeable future. The increase in the fertility rate from 1945 to 1960 was due to the cataclysmic experiences of World War II and the Great Depression and is unlikely to reoccur. The more recent decline in the fertility rate is a resumption of a long-term trend since 1800, and social developments in recent years are likely to reinforce this trend. Attitudes toward marriage and children have changed dramatically, resulting in a declining marriage rate. At the same time, the divorce rate has been skyrocketing. Women are choosing to spend more time at work instead of at home raising children. As more and more women move into highly paid professional positions, the cost of taking time off to have and raise children is increasing sharply. People have also come to prefer the higher standards of living associated with smaller families. Birth control methods have become more effective and available. All of these trends would tend to keep the fertility rate low or depress it still further, while there seem to be few if any strong social trends tending to reverse the decline in fertility.

unless tax rates are increased from current levels. By 2040 the same Board of Trustees projections indicate that there could well be 70 beneficiaries per 100 workers. This 125 percent increase implies that at today's tax rates, taxes will be sufficient to finance only 44 percent of the expected benefits at that time. Thus, these demographic trends portend enormous financing problems for the social security program.

The Trust Funds

If social security were supported by a fully funded trust fund, in other words, if the program were run on an invested basis with each taxpayer's payments being saved and invested for his own retirement, these potential bankruptcy problems would not exist. The maturity of the program would not make financing any more difficult or precarious, because the initial generation of workers would have saved enough assets to finance their own retirement benefits. Since the taxes that current retirees had paid would always have been saved for their own retirement and the taxes of current workers would be for *their* own retirement, the decline in the fertility rate and changing demographics would not be a problem. With benefits ensured by a trust fund, rather than by current workers, benefits would not be threatened by unemployment or by sluggish wage growth. Obviously a fully funded trust fund would make social security benefits much more secure than they are now. There would always be sufficient funds saved up and on hand to finance future benefit entitlements.

As we saw earlier,[7] however, the current social security trust funds contain less than 1 percent of the amount necessary to guarantee future benefits on a fully funded basis. Social security is, therefore, clearly bankrupt by conventional accounting standards. But it is argued that social security does not need a trust fund and is not bankrupt because, unlike a private insurance company, the government can compel future workers to enter into the program and pay sufficient taxes to meet all benefit obligations. Thus social security cannot go into bankruptcy, because future benefits are ensured by the government's power to tax.

This argument, though widely accepted, is seriously deficient. It ignores the fact that because we live in a democracy and not a benevolent dictatorship, the taxing power is subject to the will of the electorate. Taxpayers retain the power through their elected representatives to refuse to continue to support benefit payments at expected levels or to end their participation in the program altogether. As noted earlier,

[7]See chap. 2.

the U.S. Supreme Court has in fact already held that taxpayers, through their elected representatives, have this power.[8] Thus the benefit payments of social security are really not any more secure than the benefit payments of a private insurance company without a trust fund, since in both cases those paying into the system can decide to stop. It makes no sense, therefore, to say that the future social security benefits are ensured by the government's power to tax, unless it is assumed that if taxpayers should decide to refuse to support such benefits, democracy will be suspended.

Therefore, what really determines whether social security is bankrupt is whether taxpayers will be willing to support the projected tax burdens necessary to finance all future benefit obligations. The real issue over whether a trust fund is necessary is whether the additional security provided by such a fund, above the taxing power, is prudently required to guarantee all expected benefit payments and prevent bankruptcy.

Will Taxpayers Continue to Pay?

In evaluating the likelihood of continued taxpayer support, one must understand just how heavy the future tax burden will be if all expected benefits are to be paid. One of the most recent projections of this future tax burden was provided in the Social Security Board of Trustees 1982 Annual Report.[9] Assuming basically a continuation of current fertility trends, the report indicates that by 2030, when most young people entering the work force today will be receiving their retirement benefits, the payroll tax rate will have to be increased to 22.63 percent to finance all benefit obligations under the OASDI portion of the program alone.[10] This compares with an OASDI payroll tax rate today of about 10 percent. The Trustees' reports do not project the costs for the HI program this far into the future. But by 2005, the necessary HI tax rate was already projected to be 11 percent under Alternative III assumptions. This compares with an HI tax rate of about 2½ percent today. The tax rate for the entire program by 2030 under these assumptions would therefore have to be at least 33 percent. Even under more optimistic assumptions, the necessary payroll tax rate was projected to be 16.83 percent in 2030.[11] Moreover, the HI program under these assumptions would

[8]See chap. 2.

[9]Social Security Board of Trustees, *1982 Annual Report of the Board of Trustees of the Federal Old-Age and Survivors Insurance and Disability Insurance Trust Funds* (Washington, D.C., April 1, 1982).

[10]These were the assumptions under Alternative III of the report. See footnote 3.

[11]Alternative IIB assumptions, *1982 Annual Report.*

already require a tax rate by 2005 of 7 percent. A. Haeworth Robertson, a former chief actuary of the Social Security Administration, has projected under similar assumptions that the HI tax rate by 2025 would have to be 8 percent.[12] The tax rate for the entire program under these assumptions would therefore have to be about 25 percent. Overall, therefore, in order to pay the benefits being promised to young workers entering the work force today, it can be expected that tax rates will have to be increased to 25-33 percent of taxable payroll.[13]

Moreover, these official projections fail to take into account the negative economic effects likely to be caused by such high social security tax rates themselves. It seems likely that a payroll tax rate of 25 percent or more will greatly discourage employment. Savings and capital investment are also likely to be further discouraged, as discussed in chapter 3, leading to fewer jobs, higher unemployment, and lower real-wage growth. The result is that revenues will not be increased as much as expected from these high tax rates, and these rates will therefore have to be raised further. The substantially lower national income and economic growth resulting from the reduced savings, capital investment, and employment will further decrease the likelihood that taxpayers will be willing to pay these necessary tax rates.

Indeed, as we have noted, we could well reach a point where higher tax rates will fail to yield higher tax revenues, because of the negative economic effects resulting from these rates. At this point, the economy will simply not be capable of supporting the burden of social security benefit promises, and it won't matter what tax rates taxpayers are willing to pay.

But even apart from these possibilities, the specter of social security payroll taxes alone consuming one fourth to one third of the incomes of most Americans should be frightening. The most reasonable political judgment appears to be that taxpayers will not be willing to support this enormous tax burden. People have other things they want to do with their lives besides pay taxes.

As a result, the social security program will not be able to meet all its future benefit obligations and can therefore be considered bankrupt. Young workers entering the program today cannot count on receiving all the social security benefits currently being promised to them, and they should not make their future plans assuming they will. It is a

[12]A. Haeworth Robertson, *The Coming Revolution in Social Security* (McLean, Va.: Security Press, 1981), chap. 4.

[13]After a detailed review of other official projections, the same conclusion was reached in Ferrara, *Social Security: The Inherent Contradiction*, chap. 5.

scandal that these promised benefits are not only inferior to those available through private alternatives, but are also unlikely ever to be paid.

Since a fully funded social security trust fund would eliminate the vulnerability of social security benefits to the desires of future taxpayers, simple prudence would lead to the conclusion that such a trust fund is necessary to adequately guarantee future benefits and prevent bankruptcy. This trust fund, however, need not be held by the government. It could instead be held by citizens in the form of individual retirement accounts.

Conclusion

In response to a question concerning social security during the 1980 presidential debates, Jimmy Carter stated:

> [A]lthough there was a serious threat to the social security system and its integrity during the 1976 campaign and when I became President, the action of the Democratic Congress working with me has been to put social security back on a sound financial basis. That's the way it will stay.[14]

Voice-stress analyzers reviewing the debate noted that Jimmy Carter's voice pattern showed the most stress during this statement. They concluded that Jimmy Carter was lying.

Jimmy Carter *was* lying. His own official government reports showed that tax rates would have to be increased to politically unacceptable levels to finance future benefit promises and that serious financing problems would develop as early as 1983.[15]

It is unconscionable that government officials and ardent defenders of social security are irresponsibly encouraging young people today to ignore these problems and to rely on benefit promises that are unlikely ever to be fulfilled. There is nothing humanitarian about leaving the basic financial security of future generations vulnerable to potential bankruptcy. Failure to adequately consider these problems may end

---

[14]*New York Times*, October 29, 1980.

[15]Both of these elements are clearly indicated in the 1982 Annual Trustees' Reports, as we have seen in this chapter. But they were also indicated in the 1980 Annual Trustees' Reports issued during Carter's term. See Social Security Board of Trustees, *1980 Annual Report of the Board of Trustees of the Federal Old-Age and Survivors Insurance and Disability Insurance Trust Funds* (Washington, D.C., June 17, 1980); Social Security Board of Trustees, *1980 Annual Report of the Board of the Federal Hospital Insurance Trust Funds* (Washington, D.C., June 17, 1980).

up hurting most the very people social security's strongest advocates seek to help.

The problems we have discussed in this chapter are not remote or speculative. They are of immediate concern. Taxpayers, especially young taxpayers, are being asked to continue to pay large amounts in taxes and to base their financial plans on the promise of future benefits. They need to know, therefore, how reliable these benefit promises are. Furthermore, the social and economic factors causing the financial difficulties of social security are strong, basic forces in American life today, not remote speculations. These factors are causing serious financial problems for the program now as well as in the future.

These problems are all due to the conflict between the welfare and insurance objectives of the program. They all result from the operation of the program on a pay-as-you-go basis. As we have seen, this method of operation resulted from the pursuit of welfare objectives in the early years of the program, which has made it an unstable, financially insecure insurance program. Once again, the solution to this problem is to separate the welfare and insurance objectives of the program and to rely on private, invested alternatives to perform the insurance function.

VI. Social Security and Minorities

Many believe that one of the chief purposes of social security is to help the weakest and most vulnerable groups in our society. Indeed, this is one of the prime reasons for the strong public support of the program in the past.

But the truth is that social security discriminates against some of the nation's most vulnerable minority groups, especially the poor, blacks, and women. Moreover, these groups can least afford the negative effects resulting from the program's other problems. As a result, the program hurts most the very people many of its supporters are trying to help.

It is true that the welfare aspects of social security are quite helpful to some of these groups, but these same welfare benefits can be provided through alternative programs or institutions without the discrimination and negative effects of social security. Social security hurts these groups by preventing them from fully enjoying the benefits they are meant to enjoy.

A Structural Problem

Discrimination against minorities and individuals who follow alternative lifestyles is built into the structure of the program. Social security forces everyone to participate in one big insurance program with one particular pattern of coverage and benefit provisions. This pattern of coverage and benefits is geared to the circumstances and characteristics of the individuals who predominate in society and who, therefore, constitute the politically powerful majority. The program's provisions will deviate from this norm only to provide special accommodation to groups with disproportionate political power.

Members of minority groups, however, tend to have circumstances and characteristics that deviate from the norm. Also, they do not possess substantial political power. Consequently, they will find that the uniform coverage and benefit provisions of the government's social security program are poorly suited to their needs and preferences. The result is that social security will invariably hurt minority groups by forcing participation in an insurance program that does not serve their true needs. The same problems will plague individuals who pursue alternative lifestyles, who also tend to have special circumstances and characteristics, yet lack unusual political power.

The Poor

Social security discriminates against the poor in several important respects.[1] Poorer individuals tend to start working earlier in life than those in higher income classes, but social security credits these individuals with few, if any, additional benefits for these additional years of work and tax payments. The poor also tend to die earlier than those in higher income classes, and therefore they receive less in benefits. Social security taxes self-employed individuals at a lower rate, yet the poor are far less likely to be self-employed than those in the higher-paying professions. Single, unattached individuals are much more likely to be poor than married couples, yet social security provides additional benefits for married couples. Finally, social security benefit amounts are based on an average of one's past earnings, but the five years of lowest earnings are deleted from the calculation. This benefits most those whose earnings will increase the most over the course of their lives, which is likely to be those in the higher income brackets.

These discriminatory elements all add up to one result—the poor pay more for less.[2] A study by Henry J. Aaron of the Brookings Institution[3] concluded that because of these factors the poor receive a lower return in retirement benefits on their past tax dollars than those with higher incomes, despite the substantial welfare elements in the program that are designed to give them a higher return. The effectiveness of these welfare elements therefore is entirely outweighed by the program's discriminatory elements.

Social security hurts the poor in several other important ways. The program's payroll tax is regressive, taking a higher percentage of the incomes of those at lower income levels. While a standard fee analogous to the payroll tax is an appropriate way to charge for a service such as insurance protection, the welfare benefits paid through social security are also financed by the program's regressive payroll tax. This method of financing welfare benefits is counterproductive, since the burden of the tax falls most harshly on the very income groups the welfare ele-

---

[1] For a more detailed discussion of the program's discriminatory and negative effects on the poor, as well as on other minority groups, see Peter J. Ferrara, *Social Security: The Inherent Contradiction* (San Francisco: Cato Institute, 1980), chap. 6.

[2] This effect of the program has been emphasized by Nobel laureate Milton Friedman in numerous publications and forums. For one of his most comprehensive discussions of the problem, see Wilbur J. Cohen and Milton Friedman, *Social Security: Universal or Selective?* (Washington, D.C.: American Enterprise Institute, 1972).

[3] Henry J. Aaron, *Demographic Effects on the Equity of Social Security Benefits* (Washington, D.C.: Brookings Institution, 1979).

ments are supposed to help. Social security, then, hurts the poor by coupling welfare benefits meant to help them with an inappropriate, regressive means of financing.

Social security also wastes many welfare benefits on those who are not poor. Welfare benefits are not paid on the basis of need as measured by a means test, but instead on the basis of other factors that are very inadequate measures of true need. Thus many who are not in need are nevertheless able to qualify for these generous welfare subsidies.

The clearest example of this problem is "double-dipping" by government employees who are covered by special government pension programs rather than social security. These workers will often work the minimum amount of time in the private sector that they need in order to qualify for social security benefits in addition to their government pensions. Their sparse private earnings history will then qualify them for the social security welfare subsidies meant for poor workers who do not have a second pension.

Similar problems arise from the payment of additional benefits for the dependents of workers. As we saw in chapter 2, additional retirement, survivors', disability, and health insurance benefits are available to a worker if he has a spouse, young children, or other dependents, even though he may not have paid any more in taxes than a worker who retires without such dependents. These provisions are based on the welfare rationale that an individual with dependents is more likely to be needy than an individual without, and therefore he should receive more in benefits regardless of whether he has earned or paid for them.

Wealthy individuals have wives and children, too. In fact, families including a husband and a wife tend to be poor far less often than families with a single parent, and these families tend to be poor less often than single persons. In 1977 the median income for single individuals not living with any relatives was $8,296, with 23 percent below the poverty level, while families including both husband and wife and one-parent families (as well as families with other combinations of related individuals living together) had a median income of $21,023, with just 10 percent below the poverty level.[4] Thus the existence of a spouse and other dependents is a very poor surrogate for true need, and paying out welfare benefits on this basis will result in a substantial waste of assets meant to help the poor.

Social security's negative effects on the economy, as discussed in chapter 3, fall most heavily on the poor, who need not only the income

[4]President's Council of Economic Advisers, *1982 Economic Report of the President* (Washington, D.C.: Government Printing Office, 1982), p. 264.

lost from paying into the program, but also the new jobs and upward mobility available only in a rapidly growing economy. Similarly, the poor also most need the higher benefits available through the private, invested alternatives to social security, as we saw in chapter 4.

It should be noted also that social security causes a far more unequal distribution of wealth than would exist under the alternative, private, invested system. This is because under social security's pay-as-you-go system individuals lose the large, accumulated amounts of money each would have in their own individual retirement and insurance accounts under the private, invested system. These accounts would be quite large relative to the total amount of wealth in the economy, and the money in the accounts would be far more equally distributed than other wealth, since individuals would each be saving and accumulating fairly equal amounts in their accounts each year. The result is that, under the private system, total wealth, including the wealth in the accounts, would be far more equally distributed than is currently the case under social security. Economists estimate that if individuals saved and invested in their own retirement and insurance accounts all that they currently pay in social security taxes, over 40 percent of the nation's wealth would be held in this widely distributed form and the nation's concentration of wealth would be reduced by at least one third.[5]

Blacks

Since a higher proportion of blacks are poor than of other social groups, all the negative effects of social security on the poor apply particularly to them. Two of these effects are especially pronounced.

First, unemployment is more widespread among blacks, especially teenage blacks, than among other social groups. Social security, by discouraging saving and capital investment, keeps this unemployment much higher than it would otherwise be, given our current economic structures.

---

[5]Martin Feldstein, "Social Security, Induced Retirement and Aggregate Capital Accumulation," *Journal of Political Economy* 82 (September/October 1974); Feldstein, "Social Security and the Distribution of Wealth," *Journal of the American Statistical Association,* December 1976.

This discussion should not be taken to imply support for government policies of income redistribution away from the rich and toward the poor. If individuals earn their wealth and income through productive activity and free and voluntary exchanges in the market, then it is really not any of the government's business how much each citizen has. But when the result of active and unnecessary government intervention in this process is to increase the concentration of wealth, then there is a basis for legitimate complaint.

Second, the mortality tables show that life expectancy among blacks is the lowest of any social groups, even lower than the poor in general. The expected retirement benefits for young blacks are therefore much lower than for young whites. These lower benefits represent a much lower return on the taxes paid by blacks than on the taxes paid by whites.[6]

Women

The benefit provisions of social security are based on a traditional view of the family, with the husband as wage earner, the wife as homemaker, and numerous children. This underlying model is the primary source of the program's pervasive and systematic discrimination against women.

The program in particular discriminates against women who are single, or work, or are childless. The program provides many additional benefits to individuals with spouses and dependent minor children, yet a single or childless individual, who can never receive such benefits, must pay the same taxes. In addition, a married woman is penalized for working, in that she must either forgo the benefits she has earned on her own earnings record, and therefore receive nothing for her years of tax payments, or forgo the wife's benefits on her husband's earnings record. In the latter case, she still will receive only the difference between her own benefits and the wife's benefits, in return for her years of tax payments, as compared with a woman who does not work and, therefore, pays no social security taxes.[7] It is clear that the message from the Social Security Administration to women is: Get married, stay home, and have lots of children. Social security works less well for those whose families differ from the traditional model. Those whose lifestyles follow the traditional path receive more in benefits and a greater return on their tax dollars than those who stray from the norm. Those who do not follow traditional lifestyles are penalized and forced to subsidize those who do.

Social security has also discriminated against women by denying benefits for their husbands based on their past tax payments and earn-

[6]For a more detailed discussion of the effects of lower life expectancy on the benefits received by blacks, see Ferrara, *Social Security: The Inherent Contradiction*, chap. 6.

[7]For a more detailed discussion of these discriminatory impacts of the program, see ibid. These effects really amount to discrimination against individuals who pursue alternative lifestyles, rather than against women in particular. Yet women have been most concerned in recent years about maintaining the freedom of women to pursue these nontraditional lifestyles.

ings record, while paying benefits on the tax and earnings record of men for their wives. The U.S. Supreme Court has recently struck down some of these discriminatory provisions as unconstitutional,[8] but other, similarly discriminatory provisions remain in the program.

Welfare vs. Insurance

The harmful effects on minority groups again are due to the conflict between welfare and insurance objectives. For example, many of the welfare benefits paid through social security are wasted on the nonpoor because the program does not have a means test. The program lacks such a test because it pays out substantial insurance benefits that are considered earned by everyone who paid for them, regardless of need. Mixing welfare benefits with these insurance benefits means that the welfare benefits cannot be made subject to a means test either. Thus, the insurance elements in social security make it a wasteful welfare program.

Similarly, the program is financed by a regressive payroll tax because it is supposed to be an insurance program. This is an appropriate way to finance insurance because everyone should be charged the same price for a good or service, just as everyone is charged the same price for a loaf of bread. It is only fair that the amount paid for goods or services should depend on their value, regardless of whether the purchaser is rich or poor. But with welfare and insurance mixed in together, the result is welfare benefits financed by a counterproductive, regressive tax.

The harmful effects on the poor resulting from the program's negative impacts on the economy and its developing inferiority to private alternatives are also due to the conflict in the program's objectives, as discussed in chapters 3 and 4. In addition, the increased concentration of wealth caused by the program results from its pay-as-you-go nature that, as we have discussed earlier, is due to the pursuit of welfare objectives in the early years of the program.

Finally, the program discriminates against the poor generally by requiring them to pay more for less. This occurs because the provisions of the program are adapted to the circumstances and characteristics of the politically powerful majority, rather than those of the poor. As we have noted, this naturally results from forcing everyone to participate in one big insurance program with one particular pattern of coverage

---

[8]*Weinberger* v. *Wiesenfeld*, 420 U.S. 636 (1975); *Califano* v. *Goldfarb*, 430 U.S. 199 (1977). For a more detailed discussion of these cases and remaining discriminatory impacts of the program against women, see Ferrara, *Social Security: The Inherent Contradiction*, chap. 6.

and benefit provisions. Since this pattern is democratically chosen, it will be best adapted to the politically powerful majority, rather than members of minority groups such as the poor.

But everyone must be forced to accept the one particular pattern of benefit provisions offered by social security because of the welfare elements of the program. Because social security pursues welfare objectives in addition to insurance ones, the program must be universal and compulsory. If it were voluntary, those who were not benefiting from the welfare elements would drop out, leaving no one to pay for them. Thus, it is the welfare elements that cause social security to be a naturally discriminatory insurance program toward the poor.

The program's negative impacts on blacks are also caused by the conflict in objectives in the same way as with the poor. Similarly, all the provisions in the program that discriminate against women are based on welfare rationales. These provisions increase benefits where need is supposedly greater and decrease benefits where it is thought need may be less, regardless of past tax payments. Moreover, as long as the welfare elements require social security to impose one universal insurance program on everyone, these discriminatory elements, particularly those that discriminate against single, working women, are likely to be a continuing feature of the program. The program is likely to remain best suited to the needs and circumstances of those who adopt the traditional family model, rather than single, childless, or working women, or anyone who pursues alternative lifestyles. If the program is changed to adapt to these lifestyles, then it will be discriminatory toward those who adopt the more traditional lifestyles.

Conclusion

It should be clear that one big insurance plan with one particular pattern of coverage and benefit provisions cannot possibly meet the widely varying needs and preferences of different individuals in our society. A single person has different needs from a married childless couple, who have different needs from a married couple with several children. Working women, single or married, have different needs from nonworking homemakers and mothers. The poor need different protection from the rich; the members of various minority groups need different protection from those who make up the majority.

In a nation as diverse and pluralistic as ours, it is particularly necessary to have a system that can be individually adapted to varying needs. This can be accomplished only through a private insurance system. Individuals and families could then choose the one particular plan or package of insurance protection that is most suited to them from a wide variety of options and alternatives offered in the marketplace. Those with needs and preferences that deviate from the norm would especially be able to get more for their insurance dollars by pursuing options more finely tailored to their special situations.

To utilize this private, alternative system, the welfare elements of social security, again, need to be separated from the insurance elements. The insurance portion of the program could then slowly be changed to allow individuals and families to rely on the private system instead, as we will propose in chapter 10. Continuing the welfare elements in a separate program would allow minority group members to continue to enjoy the positive aspects of the current program; yet the negative and discriminatory effects of the program would be entirely eliminated.

VII. Social Security and Politics

Social security is run by the government rather than by private-market institutions, which puts the entire program in the political realm. Every question concerning the program becomes a political issue. This means that extraneous, noneconomic, and perhaps irrational political considerations will enter into the determination of how the program will be run. It means that the program will be run on a political basis rather than on an economic basis.

Operating in the political realm results in two major sets of problems. The first is that because the program is subject to political influences, there are numerous opportunities for individuals and groups to use the program to achieve their own ends at the expense of the goals of the program's participants. The second is that the nature of the political process makes it more difficult for the program's participants to effectively express their needs and preferences about its insurance goals and more difficult for the program to respond to those needs and preferences.

Politicians vs. the People

The participants in the social security program are the taxpayers and beneficiaries whose goals are to obtain insurance protection against retirement, disability, sickness, and death. Because the program is subject to political influences, however, there are at least two groups who may be able to use the program to achieve their own, quite different goals, at the expense of the participants' goals. The first group is composed of politicians and elected officials, who want to advance their political careers and get or remain elected. They may seek to achieve their goals through the social security system by operating it in a way that is politically popular in the short run but will redound to the detriment of the participants in the long run, making the achievement of the participants' goals more expensive and difficult.

Perhaps the most important example of this is the way Congress handled the trust funds in the fifties and early sixties. As we saw in chapter 2, social security was initially sold to the public on the premise that it would be operated in the same way as a private insurance program, with taxes saved and invested in a fully funded trust fund that would be used to finance the future benefits of these taxpayers. Though Congress began to move away from this fully funded approach as early as 1939, there were still enough assets in the trust funds to run the program on a fully funded basis as late as 1950.[1] But in virtually every election year for the next several years, Congress voted to increase benefits without commensurately raising taxes. The result was a precipitous decline in the relative size of the trust funds, falling from 1,343 percent of one year's benefits in 1950 to 103 percent in 1965 (see table 5). In essence, Congress simply raided the trust funds to buy votes by paying unearned benefits, completely changing the program over to a pay-as-you-go basis in the process.

The purpose of paying these unearned benefits was clearly to advance the political careers of the politicians in power by inducing the recipients to vote to keep their benefactors in office. As we have seen, however, the loss of the trust funds and the establishment of a pay-as-you-go system was seriously detrimental to the program's participants. Thus politicians used the program to advance their own goals rather than to provide efficient, reliable, and remunerative insurance.

A second category of individuals who may seek to advance their own goals instead of the participants' are members of politically powerful special-interest groups. These groups are of two types—those that seek material gain and those that seek ideological gain.

The first type may use their political power to gain special advantages in the program that will accrue to themselves at the expense of other program participants. Such a group may seek a special benefit provision that will provide extra benefits to its members. An example would be the support of blue-collar labor unions for increased benefits for spouses and children of workers. The members of such unions are more likely to follow a traditional lifestyle and will benefit most from these provisions. Groups can also seek special benefit provisions that will result in indirect gains such as an increase in customers for their particular business. An example would be the heavy support of the education industry for the benefits provided to a child of a deceased or retired worker while that child is a student over eighteen. Nonstudents over eighteen do not receive any such benefits.

The second type of group will seek to use the program not for personal monetary gain but to advance some social goal or principle even though it is irrelevant to the insurance goals of the program's

[1]The sum of $13.7 billion, which was held by the social security trust funds in 1950, was well over thirteen times one year's benefits (see table 5). This sum, if invested properly, would probably have been enough to finance all future benefit obligations of the program, if the program had then stopped accruing further benefit obligations. This is how one determines whether an insurance program is maintaining sufficient assets to operate on a fully funded basis.

participants and may detract from achieving these goals if pursued through the program. The most obvious example of this is the welfare portion of the benefit structure. Those in favor of increased welfare subsidies to various groups have used their power to pursue these goals through the social security system. They have encouraged Congress to raid the trust funds and use the saved assets to pass out free welfare subsidies. They have worked for the addition and expansion of each of the welfare elements in the program. They have even argued that social security is a good program because it allows them to use their influence to gain a surreptitious distribution of welfare benefits that the public would not support if attempted in the open.[2] We have already seen in detail, however, how the mixing of the welfare and insurance elements has ruined the insurance portion of the program for taxpayers and beneficiaries.

Politics vs. the People

The second set of difficulties arises because of the cumbersome nature and bad incentive structure of the political process itself.

If a taxpayer or beneficiary wants a change in his insurance coverage under the program to better suit his needs and preferences, he must act through cumbersome political channels. He must, in effect, start a national political movement to bring about the desired change. He must gain national attention amidst the whole range of public policy issues competing for such attention. He must convince others of the validity of the change. He must be able to exert enough national political pressure to enact the change into law. Moreover, to be successful, he must amass an enormous amount of information concerning the intricate details of the program and related issues, become an expert in the relevant academic disciplines such as economics and demography, and develop the political skills necessary to carry on a national campaign.

Further complicating this task is the fact that virtually everyone is forced to participate in social security and therefore to accept the one particular pattern of coverage and benefit provisions that the program offers. Since a change that is well suited to the needs and preferences of some individuals is likely to be ill suited to the differing needs and preferences of others, there will always be a natural political constituency to oppose such changes.

In addition, because social security is a bureaucratic institution operating through the political process, rather than a private institution

[2]See discussion in Milton Friedman, *Capitalism and Freedom* (Chicago: University of Chicago Press, 1962), pp. 184–85.

operating through a market process, the administrators have little incentive to make changes according to the needs and preferences of taxpayers and beneficiaries. The Social Security Administration does not have to worry about selling additional social security "policies" to stay in business; everyone is already forced to participate. Moreover, the administering bureaucrats cannot gain any profit or other financial reward from changing social security to make it a better product; they consequently face only the risk of arousing political opposition by advocating such changes.

Even if SSA did want to improve the program, it could not just make the change and test it in the marketplace as a private-market institution could. It would have to take its case to Congress just like everyone else. It would have to start a national political movement, or perhaps a major political controversy, to make the change.

Over all, the costs in time and money of making the changes in the program that an individual may need or prefer will undoubtedly outweigh the changes' benefits to him. And government officials in charge of the program are unlikely to initiate such changes. Efforts for change, therefore, will probably never develop, and the program will stagnate, matching poorly the needs and preferences of taxpayers and beneficiaries.[3]

The Market Alternative

The situation described above contrasts sharply with the provision of insurance protection through private-market institutions. Instead of launching a national political movement, an individual in a private-market system can satisfy his needs and preferences merely by purchasing, from a wide variety of options available in the marketplace, the investment and insurance plan of protection that is best suited to him. If an individual desires to make a change, he need only change his purchases or otherwise rearrange his financial affairs. He need not call a press conference or hold congressional hearings. He does not need to convince others that his plan is right or that he has some special claim to justice. He only needs to know his own affairs and desires and what is available in the marketplace, which private companies will not keep a secret. There would be no conflict between individuals, because

[3]This stagnation seems to have occurred with the current program. For example, as we saw in chapter 6, the program's benefit structure was built on a concept of the traditional family that is far less typical today than it was in the 1930s. Yet despite the great social changes since that time, changes in the program to match these trends have been slow or nonexistent.

each would be free to purchase the package of insurance and investment options that best suited him personally.

Private-market institutions would also have an incentive to model their products according to the needs and preferences of consumers and to alter their products to keep pace with changes in these needs and preferences. The continued income of a private company is solely contingent on the degree to which the firm's products match the needs and preferences of consumers. Well-designed products will result in immediate financial reward to the company and its employees. The result is therefore likely to be a diverse, flexible, adaptable, and fluid array of insurance and investment options offered to customers.

Finally, private-market institutions would not be subject to the same corrupting political influences as social security since they would not be public bureaucracies operating in the political realm. Politicians and special-interest groups would not have the same ability to commandeer these institutions for their own ends. Indeed, these institutions would have to strenuously resist distraction from their insurance goals or else they might be unable to attract sufficient customers to stay in business.

Conclusion

Again, these problems are all due to the conflict between the welfare and insurance objectives of the program. They arise only because social security is operated by the government and is subject to the influences and difficulties inherent in the political process. But since the program contains welfare elements which make the program unremunerative for those who will not benefit from them, the government must run the program and force everyone to participate.

Thus, because welfare and insurance are mixed, the insurance elements become subject to numerous political instabilities and difficulties. These problems are easily solved by simply separating the welfare and insurance functions into separate programs and privatizing or denationalizing the insurance function.

VIII. Social Security and Liberty

A basic characteristic of social security is that it is compulsory and based on coercion: All individuals are forced to participate regardless of their preferences. If one feels that he has better uses for his own money, he cannot voluntarily opt out of the program and forgo both taxes and benefits; there are heavy legal penalties, including fines and imprisonment. Thus, social security is not based on the voluntary consent of the individual participants, but on coercion.

With social security currently consuming over 13 percent of taxable payroll, and this likely to increase to 25 percent or more over the next forty years, the program's coercive and compulsory nature must be considered a serious restriction on the freedom of American citizens to run their own lives and enjoy the fruits of their own labor. The program mandates that one-eighth to one-fourth of the incomes of most Americans will be used for one purpose and that this purpose will be pursued by one means—participation in social security. Thus Americans are denied the freedom to control a major portion of their own incomes. They are also denied the freedom to choose alternative means of pursuing the insurance goals of social security.

Such a serious restriction on individual liberty ought to be viewed as a major drawback of any program or public policy, but this is particularly true with regard to a program like social security where the same insurance goals of the program can be achieved through private-market institutions.

It is hard to understand why many who profess great concern for individual liberty have not been concerned over this serious loss of liberty. The loss of control over a major portion of one's income is at least as significant to the average American as infringements on freedom of speech or any of the other freedoms that command great respect in our system of government.

Unfortunately, in recent decades most intellectuals seem to have entirely forgotten the major portion of America's heritage of liberty. These thinkers have focused great attention on freedom of speech and of the press, on freedom of assembly and the right to petition government, on the freedom to choose one's own lifestyle, and other civil rights, all clearly of great importance in any free society. But they have completely ignored freedom in the economic realm. The freedom to buy, sell, trade, work, make contracts, own and use property, enjoy the fruits of one's own labor (including freedom from confiscatory and excessive taxation), and similar economic rights should receive the same respect as other civil rights. These economic freedoms deal with issues that are the real, daily concerns of the great majority of individuals and therefore as important as any other rights. Moreover, historically they have been the central focus of the American conception of liberty rather than a secondary concern.

Social security's restriction of liberty is an infringement on these important economic rights. It is time that this restriction became recognized as a significant problem and that it be modified or eliminated.

We can break down the various elements of coercion in the insurance portion of social security into an analytical framework similar to one advanced by Milton Friedman.[1] These elements are:

(a) the requirement that individuals make some provision for their old age and other contingencies;

(b) the requirement that this provision be made by buying one type of insurance—social security; and

(c) the requirement that this one type of insurance be purchased from one "seller"—the federal government.

If *any* of these elements are eliminated, freedom and individual liberty will be increased even though the other elements remain. Even if individuals are required by the government to accept element (a) and make some provision for their retirement and other contingencies, freedom will still be increased if individuals are allowed to opt out of social security and pursue this goal by alternative means of their own choice. This would eliminate elements (b) and (c). In essence, individuals would be freer if the retirement insurance business (and other forms of insurance provided by social security) were denationalized and they could choose their own insurance plans. This is analogous to the voucher proposal for public education. The voucher proposal would still require individuals to use certain amounts of their income to educate their children, but it would allow them to choose the school and type of eduction for their children that they desire, increasing individual liberty.

Conclusion

The problems discussed in this chapter are, once again, due to the conflict between welfare and insurance objectives. These problems all exist because the program is compulsory. As we have noted in the

---

[1] Milton Friedman, *Capitalism and Freedom* (Chicago: University of Chicago Press, 1962), p. 183.

earlier chapters, however, the program must be compulsory only because it contains welfare elements. As a result, some participants receive more in benefits than the value of their past taxes, and others receive less. If the program were not compulsory, all those who did not receive the benefit of the welfare provisions would opt out, leaving no one to pay for them. The program would then go into bankruptcy. If the welfare elements were split off from social security and put into a separate program, social security could then be made completely voluntary, and the problems discussed here could be substantially eliminated.

IX. Social Security and Justifications

We have seen that the social security program has numerous serious shortcomings. But if the program is so bad, why do we have it? Is there any convincing justification for it? Does the program have positive attributes that outweigh the negative?

Inadequate Justifications

Perhaps the most popular argument for social security is that without the program people simply will not provide for their retirement and other insurance contingencies. Therefore, they must be forced to do so through social security so that they and/or their families will not suffer from poverty in their old age or as a result of misfortunes earlier in life. It is hard to believe that the same people who engage in the countless daily transactions necessary to create and maintain the most complex, productive, highly technological economy in the world cannot understand the value of deferring current consumption for greater future enjoyment and are therefore incapable of providing for their retirement and other contingencies on their own. There is certainly no developed body of empirical evidence to support this view. The existence of a large and thriving private insurance business in this country suggests that the argument is entirely fallacious.

In any event, this argument is based on the highly objectionable, paternalistic premise that the government has the right to force individuals to take certain actions for their own good. Such paternalism would seriously restrict the freedom of individuals to control their own lives and pursue their own goals merely because others think they are mistaken. It would allow certain elites, who think they know the one right way to live, to impose their values on everyone. It would ultimately justify totalitarian control over the lives of individuals to ensure that their every action redounds "to their own good." Individuals should be free to run their own lives according to their own tastes and desires. If some people believe that others are living their lives in error, then they have the right to try to persuade them that a mistake is being made. But they have no right to compel them to change their ways.

Ultimately, however, this forced-saving argument is simply silly as a justification for social security because on its own terms it fails to justify anything like the current program. It most justifies a simple requirement that all individuals save some portion of their income for retirement and other contingencies, but not necessarily through social security. Individuals could instead be allowed to take advantage of private alternatives, just as drivers in most states are required to carry car insurance, but can purchase it from private insurers. Replacing social security with such a simple requirement would eliminate virtually all of the negative effects that we have discussed.[1]

Another variant of this forced-saving argument is that individuals must be forced to save through social security, not for their own good, but to prevent them from imposing costs on others. These are the costs of having to finance welfare benefits in retirement and other circumstances for those who could have saved and bought insurance but did not. This argument is based on the peculiar notion that those who provide charity to some individuals have the right to restrict the liberty of third parties who are not even recipients, to ensure that they do not become recipients.

This notion is again quite objectionable philosophically. The improvident, in failing to save and consequently ending up in difficult circumstances, are not imposing costs on others. The givers of charity remain free to give or withhold to those in these circumstances. It is their decision to give that results in the costs, and if they are unhappy with these costs, they should reduce their giving. The decision to give is certainly no justification for restricting the liberty of others.

Ultimately, however, this variant of the forced-saving argument is inadequate for the same reason as the first variant. It justifies only a simple requirement that individuals make some provision for retire-

---

[1]A related rationale for social security is that it may aid in income redistribution. An income redistribution goal differs from a welfare goal in that the latter seeks to provide minimum benefits to the poor while the former seeks to equalize incomes by taxing the above average and granting benefits to the below average, even though the recipients may not actually be poor.

It is hard to justify the program on this rationale because its effect is probably to increase rather than decrease the concentration of income and wealth, as discussed in earlier chapters. Moreover, because of the insurance elements, much if not most of the program's benefits are paid to those with above-average incomes. The insurance elements would consequently make the program a very inefficient income redistribution vehicle.

Moreover, this rationale again does not justify all the elements of the program—in particular, the insurance elements. There is no reason why we should be pursuing income redistribution goals through an insurance program. If we want to redistribute income, we can have an income redistribution program. That does not mean that we should force the entire population into a social security program that attempts to provide people with insurance services.

Finally, there is no reason why the government should be pursuing income redistribution goals in the first place. If those with higher incomes have earned them through productive effort and free exchanges in the marketplace, they are entitled to keep them. Each person is entitled to the value of what he or she creates or produces.

ment and other contingencies, but not necessarily through social security.

Another possible rationale for social security is that it provides much-needed benefits to the poor. We have already noted, however, the many ways in which social security is a bad vehicle for providing welfare benefits. These welfare benefits could be provided without the drawbacks through a separate program that would provide means-tested benefits to the elderly poor and others out of general revenues. The need to provide these welfare benefits justifies only this type of program. It does not justify forcing the entire population into a social security program that pays benefits with little regard to actual need. It does not justify the insurance elements of social security. Paying welfare benefits through such a social security program only detracts from the effectiveness and efficiency of those benefits.

It is sometimes argued that social security is an ideal way to pursue welfare goals because it allows the government to pay welfare benefits without a means test. It is considered degrading to require the poor to divulge intimate details of their lives to welfare officials to prove that they are truly needy, and to be subject to check-ups to make sure that they have not lied.

But is it too much to ask of an individual who seeks welfare that he prove that he is really needy? Why should he be entitled to such benefits without such proof? How can anyone conceivably be so arrogant as to demand that the taxpayer pay out his hard-earned money indiscriminately to whoever has the audacity to ask for it?

Economic value does not fall like manna from heaven; it must be created or produced. One who asks for welfare benefits is asking that he be given value that was produced by others. He is asking that he be allowed to enjoy the fruits of someone else's labor, that he be allowed to live at the expense of others. Anyone who asks for such a privilege should at least have to prove some unusual circumstances that would make this privilege absolutely necessary. It would be unfair to those who have earned and produced what they have to demand that they hand it over to others who have shown no good reason to receive it.

As we have seen, paying welfare benefits without a means test results in the waste of a substantial portion of such benefits on those who are not poor. The waste of these benefits is unfair both to taxpayers and to the actually poor.

A means test is therefore not an unfair burden on welfare recipients, but is in fact a necessary element of any welfare program, for reasons of both equity and efficiency. Opposition to means tests in welfare programs is totally unreasonable and should receive far less serious consideration than it does today.

Still another possible rationale for social security is based on its pay-as-you-go method of operation. If such a system were actually superior to an invested system, then social security would be justified, since a pay-as-you-go system can only be provided through a government program.

The circumstances under which a pay-as-you-go system would appear to be superior to an invested system were explored originally by Nobel laureate Paul Samuelson in 1958.[2] As we discussed in chapter 4, over time the taxes collected in a pay-as-you-go system at fixed rates on payrolls would naturally grow by the rate of growth in real wages plus the rate of growth in population. Consequently, under such a system a rate of return in benefits can be paid equal to the sum of these two rates.[3] This is known as the social insurance paradox.[4] Somehow, all individuals under such a system seem to receive a positive return when the sum of the two rates noted above is positive, even though the system does nothing to increase productivity or national income. When the sum of the two rates is greater than the rate of return on capital, the pay-as-you-go system would in fact appear to be superior to an invested system.

But as we have seen, the sum of these two rates is not anywhere near the rate of return on capital, and it is highly unlikely that it will ever be. The real before-tax return to capital in the United States is over 12 percent. By contrast, the rate of growth in real wages has historically been about 2 percent and in the past three decades has been approximately 1.3 percent or even less.[5] Similarly, fertility rates have already fallen well below the rate for zero population growth, and unless these trends are sharply reversed, the population will eventually begin to decline rather than grow. A declining population could easily make

[2]Paul Samuelson, "An Exact Consumption-Loan Model of Interest With or Without the Social Contrivance of Money," *Journal of Political Economy*, December 1958, pp. 467–482.

[3]These two elements, the rate of growth in real wages and the rate of population growth, constitute the social security rate of return discussed in chapter 4.

[4]A precise mathematical presentation of this paradox was provided by Henry J. Aaron of the Brookings Institution in 1966. See Henry J. Aaron, "The Social Insurance Paradox," *Canadian Journal of Economics* xxxii (February–November 1966): 371–374.

[5]In a recent study, Professor Feldstein estimated that from 1946 to 1975 the pre-tax real rate of return on invested capital was 12.4 percent. See Martin Feldstein, "National Saving in the United States," Harvard Institute of Economic Research, Discussion Paper no. 506, October 1976.

the pay-as-you-go rate of return negative. Even if population growth returned to its historical rate of about 2 percent, the total pay-as-you-go rate of return would still be less than one third of the invested return.

Moreover, as also discussed in chapter 4, this pay-as-you-go rate of return is entirely different from the invested system's rate of return. The private, invested system is based on wealth creation. The return paid under this system comes from the increased production resulting from the investment of the funds paid into the system. Thus the rate of return in an invested system is self-financing. It does not constitute a burden on anyone. The pay-as-you-go system, by contrast, does nothing to increase production. It is instead based on mere income redistribution. Any positive rate of return paid through such a system is merely generated by increased taxes. Since there is no increased production to pay for this return, it constitutes a net burden on current taxpayers. Through this return, benefit recipients are being made better off only by making taxpayers worse off.

The returns under the two systems therefore are not at all comparable. Even if the putative returns under the two systems were exactly the same, workers in the pay-as-you-go system would have to pay extra amounts to finance the pay-as-you-go return. The return in the invested system, however, would be financed by the increased wealth produced by the system's investments, saving the workers these extra amounts.[6] Indeed, whatever the level of the pay-as-you-go return, individuals in that system would still be losing the full amount of the extra wealth that would have been created by the invested system, or the full rate of return in the invested system. Consequently, as long as this return is greater than zero, the invested system is superior, regardless of the level of the so-called pay-as-you-go rate of return.

There are other drawbacks to the pay-as-you-go system as well. Since the benefits in such a system depend on the continued payments of current workers, rather than on the saved assets of the retirees, the working generation cannot stop paying into the system for any reason. The retired generation has been induced to rely on these continued payments, and its members will be subject to extreme hardship if the payments are not made.

In a private, fully invested system, by contrast, workers could decide to stop paying into their retirement funds if they had more urgent and important uses for their contributions. Current retirees would be unaf-

[6]For a more detailed discussion of this point, see chap. 4.

fected, as their benefits would continue to be paid out of their saved assets. At the same time, current workers would be made better off, as they would be putting their available resources to the best use. But once locked into a restrictive pay-as-you-go system, workers could not make this choice.

The availability of this option could be critical in certain circumstances. If the nation were embroiled in a war, for example, funds might be urgently needed to prevent conquest, defeat, or domination by the enemy. With a fully invested system, the current working generation could suspend payments into the system and devote funds to the war effort. The only result would be a decreased retirement income, which could be made up after the war. But with a pay-as-you-go system, payments could not be diverted to the war effort, without imposing extreme hardship on the current retired generation.

These considerations apply on a more individualized level as well. A particular individual may be struck by an emergency, or may come across a unique opportunity, for which funds are urgently needed. With a private, fully invested system, the individual could temporarily divert retirement contributions toward ameliorating the emergency or taking advantage of the opportunity. Pursuing this course, the individual may well be much better off, even though he will have to live with lower retirement benefits or make up the difference later. But once locked into a pay-as-you-go scheme, these options will be entirely foreclosed to him.

Given all the other major problems discussed in earlier chapters resulting from pay-as-you-go financing, it is clear that social security cannot be justified by any possible pay-as-you-go rationale.[7]

---

[7]Another argument sometimes advanced to justify social security is that the private market cannot possibly provide actuarially fair annuities. An annuity guarantees an individual a certain monthly income for the rest of his life. Without social security, individuals would use the amounts they have saved at retirement to purchase such annuities as one of the private alternatives to social security.

It is alleged, however, that an adverse selection problem will always make these annuities unfair in a private market. This is supposedly because those who expect to live longer than the average will tend to purchase such annuities more heavily than others. To the extent that these purchasers do tend to live longer, the rates charged for annuities will have to increase to reflect the fact that typical annuity purchasers tend to impose greater costs than the average person would. If an average person seeks to buy such an annuity, he will then have to pay the higher rates due to the higher costs that most purchasers of these annuities impose, but which he does not. Thus, it is argued, the average person cannot purchase private annuities at actuarially fair rates to protect him from the same old-age contingencies that social security does.

The Compact Between Generations

Failing to find an adequate justification for social security, we are left with our original question. If social security is so bad, why do we have it? The real reason we have the program is in fact quite negative and disillusioning, and hardly serves as a justification. It can be ascertained through an understanding of the pay-as-you-go nature of the program.

When a pay-as-you-go system is first imposed, we should recall, the first generation of retirees receives full benefits even though they have paid nothing in taxes. They will, therefore, support adoption of the program. This generation obtains political support for the program from members of the working generation by promising to pay them full benefits when they retire also. Since those near retirement will have to pay relatively little in taxes to receive these full benefits, they will also support the program. Only those younger workers in their twenties and early thirties, who will have to pay taxes into the system almost all of their lives, will oppose it. When this opposition is politically insufficient, a pay-as-you-go system will be adopted.

But the benefits promised to the first working generation to obtain their payments into the system are not repaid by the first retired gen-

---

Actuarially fair rates should be based on the characteristics of the group of purchasers, not on the actuarial characteristics of the population as a whole. In any insurance system, some purchasers of insurance will impose greater risks than the average purchaser and some will impose less. But as long as the rates are based on the actuarial characteristics of the average purchaser, a potential purchaser does not face actuarially unfair rates.

Moreover, without social security, virtually everyone would be purchasing annuities, assuming they were perceived as the best private retirement alternative to social security. The actuarial characteristics of purchasers would then be virtually the same as those of the population as a whole. The average person would consequently be charged rates closely reflecting the actual costs imposed by him—rates actuarially fair in any view. If many individuals were not purchasing annuities in the absence of social security, that would mean that other possible private alternatives had been found feasible. Those who thought that annuity rates were actuarially unfair could then rely on these other private alternatives.

Insurance companies of all types face the same problem today. If life insurance or auto insurance can be offered at actuarially fair rates, so can retirement annuities. Insurance companies respond to widely varying risks by trying to focus on the different characteristics that make individuals high risks such as bad health or bad driving records, and charging those individuals higher rates than the average person with average risks. There is no reason why this could not be done for retirement annuities.

Furthermore, any resulting higher costs are surely quite small compared to the massive advantages of private-sector alternatives to social security, which we saw in chapter 4.

Finally, this argument does not justify making social security compulsory. It justifies only offering it on a voluntary basis to make sure that there would be competition for private insurers who might not offer annuities on an actuarially fair basis. If these private alternatives can be shown to be superior, this rationale provides no justification for preventing individuals from taking advantage of them.

eration, which receives these payments as their own benefits. Rather, the promised benefits will be paid by the second working generation, which is generally too young to vote, or may not have been born, at the time the system is adopted.

Thus when a pay-as-you-go social security system is first adopted, the current retired generation makes a deal with the current working generation. The retired generation borrows from the working generation and puts the next working generation up as collateral. The funds for the benefits of current retirees are borrowed from current workers, but the responsibility for paying back this debt is imposed on the next working generation. In reality, this burden is public debt that won't come due until the current retired generation is gone, the current working generation is retired, and the next one enters the workforce.

This public debt is tantamount to taxation of future generations who cannot vote when the tax is imposed. The burden of this debt must be met out of the tax funds of these future generations. The tax rates to be imposed on these future generations are determined by the amount of liabilities incurred by the first retired generation when it borrows its benefits from the first working generation.

This is more than taxation without representation. The future generations are also locked into a national pay-as-you-go retirement and insurance system that leaves the economy on a permanently lower growth path and everyone with significantly less income. They are locked into a system that pays them much less in benefits than they could receive for the same amount of money through private, invested alternatives. They are locked into a system inherently vulnerable to bankruptcy and political instabilities and rigidly inflexible to individual needs and preferences. By being forced to participate in such a system, they also lose individual liberty.

The real reason we have the program is now clear. The program is in effect a means for the first generation to tax future, unrepresented generations. These future generations, however, are not only made worse off because of this taxation, but, due to the continuing negative effects of the locked-in pay-as-you-go system, are in fact made much more worse off than the first generation is made better off. This is hardly an attractive rationale for the program. The initial generation is simply taking advantage of future generations that do not yet have voices, let alone votes, to object.

Given these origins, the program can be seen as the result of an "externality" in the political realm perfectly analogous to the concept of externalities in the economic realm. This externality arises because the first generation receives the initial benefits of the program but does not pay the costs, while those who will bear the costs are not yet around to object. The true cost of the program will consequently not be taken into account, and the program will be instituted and expanded even though costs exceed benefits. This externality will thus lead to "political failure," just as externalities in the marketplace lead to market failure.

This explanation of how the program began further illustrates how it is like a Ponzi scheme or chain letter. When such devices are used, those who get into the system first make out like bandits. That is why these devices are illegal. Those who enter first get much more from those after them than they paid to get it started. They get these increased payments by fraudulently inducing larger and larger numbers of individuals to pay into the simple transfer system, thus increasing total collections to the system available to pay benefits to the initial recipients. But when the number of individuals participating in the program can no longer expand, the participants can no longer receive more than they paid in. This ultimate limitation is not explained to later participants when they are induced to enter the system.

Similarly, the first generation in a pay-as-you-go social security system benefits by getting workers after it to pay more into the transfer system than it paid in to get it started. But once this first generation receives its windfall benefits, there are no further means of expanding the system to pay above-market windfall benefits to the second generation. This ultimate limitation again is not revealed when the system is first imposed primarily because those who would be most concerned about it are not even around to vote or otherwise object.

Social security is often touted as a compact between generations. The current working generation pays benefits to the current retired generation in return for the promise of the next generation to care for it in its old age. Our discussion of the real reason we have social security reveals the true nature of this compact. A compact implies consent among all partners to the agreement. But one wonders how there can be an agreement with generations not yet around to bargain. When a social security program is begun, the current generation is on both sides of the bargaining table, representing future generations in negotiations with itself. It is not surprising that in this type of bargaining process, the absent party comes out on the short end of the deal.

In the law, when a party is on both sides of the bargaining table, representing someone in negotiations with itself, the courts will scrutinize the contract for self-dealing—any unfair advantage taken by the party over his absent adversary. The courts will void contracts where self-dealing is found because such contracts are simple fraud. The self-dealing party has represented to the absent party that it will represent the absent party's interests fairly, but then it does not.

The social security "compact between generations" is precisely such a contract corrupted with self-dealing. The first generation has taken unfair advantage of the absent, future generations. Under traditional principles of equity, therefore, the social security compact is unfair, fraudulent and voidable.

Conclusion

After examining the possible rationales for the program, one must conclude that there is no valid justification for social security. The program is simply a way for the members of the initial generation to tax future, unrepresented generations to provide free benefits to themselves, while making all future generations even worse off than they are made better off. This is hardly a sound rationale for the program.

The numerous defects and negative impacts of the program are quite pervasive and far-reaching, touching many aspects of our economic and social lives. They hurt everyone, rich and poor, young and old, black and white. They have now reached intolerable proportions.

Worst of all, they are totally unnecessary. The social security program simply represents the nationalization of a large sector of the insurance industry for no good reason. No one has ever offered a convincing rationale for why the private market cannot be allowed to operate in this area as it does in the other areas of our economy. All the justifications for the structure of the program are transparent, unconvincing, ad hoc, after-the-fact rationalizations, which clearly do not even have the committed support of their authors. It is easy to understand why. The program as it is currently structured simply makes no sense. It forces virtually all Americans to spend a major portion of their lives almost totally dependent on the government for their source of livelihood. A legitimate reason for this mindless, overwhelming expansion of the public sector has yet to be waked up.

Given the severity of the problems and the lack of a valid justification for the current structure of the program, the compelling need for fundamental reform must be apparent to all except those who think there ain't no such thing as a bad government program.

X. Social Security and Reform

Both the liberals and the conservatives are in big trouble over social security.

Social security is the liberals' program. Born of FDR and the New Deal, it is the world's largest social welfare effort. In the present crisis, the public has not forgotten all those smug, big government liberals insisting for years that the program was fundamentally and structurally sound. The liberals have to do something about social security.

The long-term reform goal for the liberals has always been to finance social security out of general revenues, eliminating the payroll tax. This would shift the program from a regressive to a progressive financing structure. Even the liberals have begun to wonder, however, why everyone, including rich, retired doctors, lawyers, and corporate executives, should be paid large government benefits out of general revenues, regardless of whether they are poor.[1] In any event, this long-term reform goal still appears politically infeasible. So as a short-term solution to the problems of social security, the liberals advocate raising payroll taxes. But the American people don't support further payroll tax increases. Moreover, simply raising taxes won't solve all the problems of the program.

The conservatives, generally in power at the present time, have the responsibility of averting a social security disaster. Special elections held soon after Ronald Reagan's sweeping 1980 victory showed the extraordinary political dangers involved in this issue.[2] The conservatives also must do something about social security.

The conservatives have always opposed general revenue financing of the program. Moreover, after their successful national campaign in 1980 on an anti-tax platform, they can't support raising payroll taxes. Their long-term reform goal has always been to privatize the program. But they appear to believe that this is still politically infeasible. Con-

---

[1]See, e.g., Nicholas Lemann, "Antisocial Security," *Washington Monthly*, January 1978; see also, "A Fair Slice From Social Security," *New York Times*, March 7, 1982, p. A26.

[2]Two special elections were held early in 1981 soon after the Reagan administration announced its social security proposals involving substantial benefit cuts. In Mississippi, a Democrat was elected by a substantial margin to replace a Republican who had resigned. Analysts gave two reasons for the Democratic victory: black concern over Reagan's stand on the Voting Rights Act, and elderly concern over the social security proposals.

Soon after this a special election was held in Ohio to fill the seat of a Republican who had died in office. The new Republican candidate just narrowly won in a district that had been represented by Republicans for 50 years. Analysts stated that the reason for the narrowness of the win was, again, elderly concern over Reagan's social security proposals.

sequently, the short-term solution of the conservatives is to cut social security benefits. But the American people don't support cuts in social security benefits. Moreover, simply cutting benefits won't solve all the problems of the program.

Fortunately, there is a solution to the social security problem that would:

(1) give both the liberals and the conservatives what they really want;

(2) solve all the major problems of the program;

(3) in all likelihood receive the broad support of the American public; and

(4) accomplish all this without raising social security taxes or cutting social security benefits.

This last element is particularly important. We can solve the problems of social security without cutting benefits. The reform advocated below will enable young people entering the work force today to have a far more prosperous and secure retirement, while at the same time maintaining the benefits on which the elderly and those near retirement have come to rely. The reform will be guided by the principle that everyone should receive at least as much in benefits as they expect to receive from the current system, while today's young workers will eventually receive much more.

The elderly have nothing to fear from this reform. Indeed, this is one of the few proposed social security reforms which does not involve cutting benefits in some fashion. The elderly will in fact be made much better off by the reform since it will solve the program's financing problems and ensure that their expected benefits will be paid. One would therefore expect and hope that the elderly and the organizations that represent them would support these changes, for their own sake and so that their children and grandchildren could have better lives.

Before discussing this reform, however, we will briefly review other major reform proposals.

Other Reform Proposals

Though social security has been perceived as politically sacrosanct, basic and fundamental reforms of the program have been proposed by a broad array of public policy analysts who have studied the program in the past decade and a half.

The Brookings Institution was one of the first to advocate basic reforms. In a major study published in 1968,[3] *Social Security: Perspectives*

[3]Joseph Pechman, Henry Aaron, and Michael Taussig, *Social Security: Perspectives for Reform* (Washington, D.C.: Brookings Institution, 1968).

for Reform, by Joseph Pechman, Henry Aaron and Michael Taussig, the authors specifically advocated separating the welfare and insurance functions of social security into two entirely separate programs. The insurance function would continue in social security, with all benefits strictly related to the amount of income each individual earned in the past. Most of the welfare elements, as discussed in chapter 2, would be eliminated. The welfare function of the program would be transferred to a negative income tax system or a comprehensively reformed public assistance program. Under this welfare portion of the system, benefits would be paid strictly according to need and would be financed out of general revenues.

The same position was taken in a study published by the Brookings Institution in 1977 entitled *The Future of Social Security,* by Alicia Munnell.[4] One important difference is that the earlier study advocated financing the insurance portion of the new system out of general revenues, as well as the welfare portion, while Munnell advocates retaining the payroll tax to finance the insurance portion.

A similar proposal was also recently advanced by the National Federation of Independent Business, authored by Stanford University Professor Michael Boskin.[5] Under the NFIB plan, retirement benefits would be based solely on the amount of payroll taxes each individual paid, plus interest earned over time on these accumulated taxes. The interest paid on these taxes would be equal to the annual average Treasury Bill rate. The Disability and Health Insurance programs of the current social security system would remain unchanged. The welfare portion would be picked up by a revamped version of the current SSI program (described in chapter 2), with benefits based solely on need and financed out of general revenues.

The basic problem with all of these reforms, however, is that they retain a government-run, pay-as-you-go insurance system. Thus, the problem of unfairness to today's young people, described in chapter 4, will not be solved. These individuals will still be able to do better with private alternatives. Moreover, these reforms would still leave us with a system that forces us to forego the huge additions to savings and capital investment that would result from a fully funded system. They would leave retirement benefits vulnerable to the bankruptcy

---

[4]Alicia H. Munnel, *The Future of Social Security* (Washington, D.C.: Brookings Institution, 1977).

[5]National Federation of Independent Businessmen, *General Explanation of NF IB Social Security Reform Proposal,* presented at "Reforming the Social Security System: An Editorial Seminar," September 21, 1981, Washington, D.C.

problems inherent in a pay-as-you-go system. Because everyone will continue to be forced into one big program, with one benefit pattern, the program will continue to be poorly suited to individual circumstances, particularly those of minority group members. Because the program will continue to be run by government, it will continue to be subject to the negative political influences discussed in chapter 7. Because the program will still be operated on a pay-as-you-go basis, it must remain coercive. Individuals could not be allowed to voluntarily opt out because there would then be insufficient revenues to meet current benefits.

A proposal attempting to avoid the drawbacks of a pay-as-you-go insurance system was advanced by the Carter Presidential Commission on Pension Policy.[6] The Commission recommended that all employers be required to establish a minimum pension system for their workers. Employers would be required to pay 3 percent of payroll for each worker into a private trust fund, where the savings would accumulate with interest until retirement. Each worker would then be able to use the funds saved for him to finance his own retirement benefits, in addition to his social security benefits.

While the Commission's proposed system would be vastly superior to social security, since it is proposed as an addition to the current system, it does nothing to solve the problems of that system. Moreover, *requiring* today's young workers to save for their retirement on top of social security, as this reform would do, is highly dubious. Because of recent changes in the social security benefit formula, the program is basically promising these workers all of the retirement income they are likely to be willing to pay for, rather than just a floor of income. If, however, workers and employers were allowed to use part of their social security taxes to finance the alternative, private system's benefits, the commission's proposed reform would lead to a tremendous improvement over the current system.

A proposal advanced by Professor Martin Feldstein goes one step beyond the above reforms; it fully recognizes the shortcomings of a pay-as-you-go insurance system.[7] In addition to separating the welfare

[6]President's Commission on Pension Policy, *Coming of Age: Toward A National Retirement Income Policy* (Washington, D.C., February 26, 1981).

[7]Feldstein has presented his reform proposals in numerous publications and articles. See Martin Feldstein, "Toward a Reform of Social Security," *Public Interest,* Summer 1975; Feldstein, "Facing the Social Security Crisis," Harvard Institute of Economic Research, Discussion Paper no. 492, July 1976; Feldstein, "Social Insurance," Harvard Institute of Economic Research, Discussion Paper no. 477, May 1976; Feldstein, "The Optimal Financing of Social Security," Harvard Institute of Economic Research, Discussion Paper no.

and insurance portions into separate programs, he would have the government run the insurance portion on a fully funded rather than pay-as-you-go basis. Each individual's tax payments would be saved in one huge, government-run trust fund, and would be used, along with the accumulated, earned interest, to finance that individual's retirement benefits. In order to continue to pay promised benefits while the full trust fund accumulates, Feldstein would sharply increase the social security payroll tax. After the trust fund was fully accumulated, which would take many years, taxes could be lowered well below currently projected rates because of the interest that could be earned by the trust fund.

While this proposal would solve some of the continuing problems associated with the above reforms, it would create new ones. The most important of these is that through the trust fund, the government would end up owning a large portion of the private economy. According to Feldstein's own calculations, this portion could be as high as 40 percent.[8] Such widespread government ownership would substantially change the character of our present economic system, based on private property ownership and competitive free enterprise. Moreover, the investments through the fund would likely become highly politicized, with politicians or other groups seeking to use the financial power behind these investments to reward or punish other groups and individuals. In particular, these investments are likely to be used as the basis to increase substantially government regulation of private businesses. As experience with other government programs teaches, government money never comes without strings attached.

Finally, one must ask what would stop politicians from raiding the trust fund, as they did in the past, to hand out free benefits? It seems that the temptation to do so would be inevitable because politicians could buy votes in the short run, and the negative consequences would only appear years later. History has shown that the government cannot be trusted to maintain such a fund.

Arthur Laffer, professor of economics at the University of Southern California, and Dr. David Ranson, a Boston consultant, go one step beyond Feldstein; they argue that once the government trust fund is

---

388, 1974; Feldstein, "Strengthening Social Security," House Ways and Means Committee, May 15, 1977; Feldstein, Summary of Testimony on Social Security, Subcommittee on Fiscal Policy, Joint Economic Committee, May 27, 1976.

[8]See Feldstein, "Toward a Reform of Social Security"; Feldstein, "Facing the Social Security Crisis"; Feldstein, "Social Insurance"; Feldstein, "The Optimal Financing of Social Security."

accumulated, individuals should be allowed to opt out of the program for private alternatives.[9] If virtually all individuals did opt out, the shortcomings of Feldstein's proposal would be eliminated, but only after the opting out was completed. The same intractable problems would exist while the trust fund was being accumulated.

In an effort to avoid these problems, other authors have sought ways to privatize the insurance portion of the program and fully fund it through the private rather than the public sector. Under a plan advanced by Warren Shore, author of *Social Security: The Fraud In Your Future*,[10] insurance companies or other financial institutions would be allowed to sign up young workers as they entered the work force for packages of retirement, life, and disability insurance coverage. The employer and employee taxes for each worker signed up would then go to the insurance company rather than to the federal government. But for every such worker, the private firm would have to take on the responsibility of providing the benefits to one new retiree.

In time, more and more current workers would be covered by the private system rather than social security as young workers opted for the superior private alternatives. Similarly, more and more current beneficiaries would be provided for through the private system. Thus, both tax revenues and benefit obligations of the government would fall. Eventually, current beneficiaries under social security would be completely phased out. At that point, young individuals entering the work force could opt for private insurance without the burden of financing an elderly beneficiary.

The problem with this intriguing proposal is that there is not likely to be sufficient funds left after paying the benefits to the retiree to finance better benefits for the young worker than he would have gotten under social security. The proposal could be modified to match three young workers with each two retirees, or even more. In addition, some of the retiree's benefits might be subsidized from general revenues. Even in these circumstances, however, it would take an adult life span for the program to be privatized. Also, insurmountable problems might be created when workers drop out of the work force to go back to school, get married, etc.

---

[9]Arthur B. Laffer and R. David Ranson, "A Proposal for Reforming Social Security," (Boston: H. C. Wainwright and Co., May 19, 1977); Laffer and Ranson, *The Social Security Problem,* unpublished manuscript.

[10]Warren Shore, *Social Security: The Fraud in Your Future* (New York: MacMillan Publishing Co., 1975).

Another proposal has recently been advanced by A. Haeworth Robertson, former chief actuary of the Social Security Administration.[11] Under Robertson's plan, the current social security system would remain as is for all workers age 45 or over and for all current beneficiaries when his proposed reform is enacted. For workers under 45 at this time, Robertson advocates that the social security payroll tax be permanently abolished. The government, however, would still pay each of these workers retirement benefits beginning at age 70, to be financed out of general revenues. These benefits would be the same for each worker, equivalent to $250 per month in 1980 but indexed to the rate of inflation.

These workers would also be able to purchase Freedom Bonds from the government at their option once they reached age 45. The value of these bonds would increase each year at the rate of inflation, but no interest would otherwise be paid on them. The bonds could be redeemed at any time after attainment of age 60 or the death of the purchaser. These workers could then supplement their retirement benefits, payable through these bonds or the general revenue grant described above, through private savings and pension plans. In another feature of his reform, Robertson proposes that benefits paid after age 70 out of private pension plans, and perhaps Individual Retirement Accounts as well, be supplemented by general-revenue-financed government payments calculated to increase these private benefits at the rate of inflation.

Apart from the survivors benefits paid under the Freedom Bonds, no other survivors benefits would be paid for workers under age 45 when the reform is enacted. These workers could instead purchase life insurance to replace these benefits. Disability benefits would be available to these workers only in the event of permanent and total disability and would be financed out of general revenues. The monthly amount of these benefits would be equal to the monthly amount of retirement benefits payable in each year. These workers could again supplement these benefits through the purchase of private disability insurance. Medicare benefits would be available to these workers after age 70, on substantially the same terms as the current program.

Robertson's proposed new system would be a sharp improvement over the current system, but there are important drawbacks. One is that it would pay a large monthly benefit to everyone after age 70 out of general revenues. There is no conceivable reason why rich, retired doctors, lawyers, business executives, and people generally not in need should receive government payments out of general taxes. It is perverse

[11]A. Haeworth Robertson, *The Coming Revolution in Social Security* (McLean, Va.: Security Press, 1981).

to tax young working people, who need their money to buy homes, feed their families, and send their children to college, merely to provide these benefits. Robertson's general revenue payments simply amount to welfare for everybody. As was discussed in chapter 9, such benefits should be paid only to those who can show unusual circumstances to justify them. Political pressure would inevitably work to push these benefits far above the levels that Robertson envisions. The availability of these benefits for retirement would also sharply reduce the retirement savings of young workers.

The same criticisms apply to Robertson's general-revenue-financed disability and health insurance benefits. For the great majority of individuals who are not poor, these same benefits can be obtained through the purchase of private disability and health insurance.

There is another potential problem with Robertson's proposal. The payroll tax would be eliminated for all those under 45, but currently expected benefits would continue to be paid to all those over 45. This means that in the first year of the reform, payroll tax revenues would be cut at least in half and the shortfall would have to be made up from general revenues. In fiscal year 1982, this would have required a general revenue subsidy of about $90 billion.[12] Moreover, in later years of the reform, payroll tax revenues would continue to decline as the exempt portion of the population continues to rise.

This means that the necessary general revenue subsidy would increase until those just over 45 at the time of the reform retire. At this point, 100 percent of currently projected social security benefits in that year would have to be financed through general revenues. The subsidy for these benefits would then decline, and eventually be eliminated, as the retired workers over 45 when the reform started died. But the general revenue subsidies for the rest of Robertson's program would offset approximately 70 percent of this reduction, maintaining large general revenue burdens indefinitely. These general revenue subsidies may be too large for the government to absorb without unacceptably high general revenue tax increases or politically infeasible government expenditure reductions.

Another approach has been advanced by James Buchanan, professor of economics at the University of Virginia,[13] with a variation by Charles

[12]Social Security Board of Trustees, *1982 Annual Report of the Board of Trustees of the Federal Old-Age and Survivors Insurance and Disability Insurance Trust Funds* (Washington, D.C., April 1, 1982); Social Security Board of Trustees, *1982 Annual Report of the Board of Trustees of the Federal Hospital Insurance Trust Fund* (Washington, D.C., April 1, 1982).

[13]James Buchanan, "Social Insurance in a Growing Economy: A Proposal for Radical Reform," *National Tax Journal*, December 4, 1968, p. 381.

D. Hobbs and Stephen C. Powlesland.[14] These authors advocate the immediate abolition of the social security payroll tax for all workers. Workers and current beneficiaries would then receive government bonds that would entitle them to benefits already accrued based on past taxes paid into the program. These accrued benefits would be paid out of general revenues.

All workers would also be required to save a portion of their incomes for retirement. They could use these savings to purchase private retirement plans or to purchase government retirement bonds. The interest on these bonds would be equal to the higher of the average rate of interest on U.S. Treasury bonds, the annual rate of growth of GNP, or under the Hobbs-Powlesland proposal, the rate of inflation. These bonds could be redeemed at retirement for an annuity that would pay monthly benefits to the bondholder for the rest of his life based on the value of the bonds at retirement. These monthly benefits could be indexed to increase at the rate of inflation. If a bondholder died before or after retirement, the widow or widower and any children would be entitled to similar monthly benefits until the surviving spouse died or the children reached adulthood.

This reform would solve most of the problems we have noted in the current social security system. A potential problem exists, however, with the government retirement bonds. If the interest rate paid on these bonds was higher than the market rate, then their purchase would not be truly voluntary. All workers would purchase the bonds and we would in effect end up with a government, pay-as-you-go, insurance system financed out of general revenues. Moreover, if the interest rate offered on the bonds was the same as the market rate, there would be no reason to offer them. If the interest rate was below market rates, the bonds would serve merely to impoverish the gullible and uninformed. Though it would be subject to this last criticism, a bond as suggested by Robertson, which merely returns the money paid for it in real terms, might be acceptable on the grounds that it would offer a government alternative to those who wanted one and taxpayers would not be subsidizing it, at least in real terms.

Another potential problem with this reform is that all current obligations of social security would have to be paid out of general revenues from the beginning. In 1982, this would have required a general revenue subsidy of $146 billion, assuming that the reform was aimed only

[14]Charles D. Hobbs and Stephen C. Powlesland, *Retirement Security Reform: Restructuring the Social Security System*, (Concord, Vt.: Institute for Liberty and Community, 1975).

at the OASDI portion of the program.[15] This subsidy would eventually decline to zero since no more social security obligations would be accrued. But in the first several years of the reform, the necessary general revenue subsidies may again be too large without unacceptably high general revenue tax increases or politically infeasible expenditure reductions. If other government spending could be reduced or eliminated to offset the necessary subsidy, this would not be a problem.

The final reform proposal to be noted is that of Nobel laureate Milton Friedman.[16] Friedman would also immediately eliminate the payroll tax for all workers and stop the accrual of further benefit obligations. Currently accrued benefit obligations to present beneficiaries would continue to be paid. Current workers would also receive a proportion of future expected benefits based on the proportion of past taxes they had paid. These remaining obligations would be financed out of general revenues. Workers could then save for their retirement and purchase insurance on their own. There would be no requirement for such savings or insurance purchases.

To pick up the welfare elements of the current system, Friedman would enact a negative income tax that would pay a subsidy to all those with incomes under a certain level, including the elderly. This subsidy would be higher the lower the income.

This reform would solve virtually all the problems we have noted without most of the drawbacks of the earlier reforms. Its reliance on the negative income tax, however, might have a detrimental impact on the incentives for lower income individuals to continue working. It might be better to rely on a revamped version of the SSI program, described in chapter 2, to perform this function. More importantly, Friedman's proposal would also have the insurmountable financing problems of the Buchanan reform, since it would also require immediate general revenue financing of all current social security obligations.

This review[17] indicates that basic, fundamental reforms of the social security program have been advocated by a wide range of prominent authors, including some of the nation's most distinguished economists and public policy analysts. All of the proposals discussed here would be an improvement over the current system, although some would be

[15]Social Security Board of Trustees, *1982 Annual Report of the Board of Trustees of the Federal Old-Age and Survivors Insurance and Disability Insurance Trust Funds,* p. 56.

[16]Wilbur J. Cohen and Milton Friedman, *Social Security: Universal or Selective?* (Washington, D.C.: American Enterprise Institute, 1972).

[17]For a more detailed discussion of the reform proposals reviewed here, see Peter J. Ferrara, *Social Security: The Inherent Contradiction* (San Francisco: Cato Institute, 1980), chap. 11.

better than others. The reform presented in the next section is a natural extension of these proposals.

A Proposal for Reform

Our analysis throughout this book suggests that the key principle behind any sensible social security reform is to separate the welfare and insurance elements of the current social security program into two entirely separate programs or sets of institutions. This would allow the insurance function to be entirely privatized—to be performed by private savings, investment, and insurance institutions in the general market. The welfare function of the program would be immediately served by an updated SSI program. A reform along these lines would solve all the major problems of the program as well as providing a number of substantial spinoff benefits.

Under any such reform, currently expected social security benefits would have to be paid with general revenues replacing the lost payroll taxes. The one problem in implementing this reform is how to pay for these benefits while allowing workers to use their social security tax money to save and invest in the private alternatives. The problem would be transitory, since remaining benefit obligations and the need to finance them would eventually be phased out. During this transition, general revenues could be used to meet these costs, but how could these revenues be raised?

These revenues should not be raised through increases in general revenue tax rates. This would put too great a burden on the working generation at the time of the reform. Nor should these revenues be raised through borrowing. Financing remaining social security obligations in this way would deprive the economy of the increased savings and capital investment that the reform should otherwise achieve.

There are a number of ways in which these remaining obligations can be financed without placing an unmanageable burden on the working generation. The most important of these is to structure the reform so as to capture some of the resulting benefits to future generations for use in financing the costs of the reform. Our discussion in chapter 9 indicated that all generations after the start-up phase of the program were made worse off as a result of it. Our reform would make these generations better off, and if the value of some of these improvements could be captured for current use, this would be an ideal means for financing the reform. Basically, the reform would create or increase wealth, and some of this new wealth could be used to pay off the costs of the reform. (One way this new wealth can be partially captured is to continue to tax some of the returns on the new investments resulting from the reform during the phase-in periods before the full tax exemption system proposed below is instituted.)

A second means for easing the financial burden of the reform is to phase it in over a number of years, if necessary. After this, the most painless way to address the remaining financing burden is to squeeze the necessary general revenues out of government resources. This would involve reducing other government expenditures to provide revenues to finance the transitory costs of the reform. It could also involve selling unused, surplus federal property.

With the reform structured to take advantage of these options, the annual general revenue expenditures that would be necessary for a number of years would be well worth the extraordinary benefits of the reform.

Preliminary Reforms

It would be useful to note a few possible, preliminary changes that would make our ultimate reform financially easier to achieve. These are not integral or necessary elements of that reform, however, and are noted here only because they seem justified on their own merits.

One is to change the current method of indexing. As discussed in chapter 2, the future benefits to be received by a worker increase at the rate of growth in wages while he is working, though these benefits increase at the rate of increase in prices after the worker becomes a beneficiary. Since wages increase faster than prices in normal times, this indexing system, adopted in 1977, means that social security benefits will grow much more rapidly in the future than if the entire system was simply indexed to prices. Because of this indexing system, social security will in the future depart even further from its original intent of providing a basic floor for retirement income, and will instead provide virtually all retirement income desired by most people. Changing over to price indexing would restrain the future growth of social security expenditures. This would ease the financial burden of our proposed reforms by reducing the transitory general revenue subsidies necessary to implement them.[18]

In recent years, however, prices have actually increased faster than wages. Though this is clearly a transitory phenomenon, it has meant that during these years the incomes of nonworking retirees have increased faster than the incomes of working people. This unusual situation can

[18]For a more detailed discussion of price indexing, see ibid., p. 314–324.

be prevented in the future by indexing benefits to the *lower* of annual price or wage increases, rather than adopting simple price indexing.

Another possible preliminary reform is to phase in a gradual delay of the retirement age from 65 to 68. This proposal has been widely advocated by numerous groups and individuals. As the work force continues to improve in health and longevity, it makes sense to delay retirement and encourage individuals to remain productive, active members of society. This would also slow the future growth of benefits, taxes, and liabilities, making long-term reform easier.

Still another possible reform is to eliminate the welfare elements in the current social security benefit structure. This would make social security benefits strictly related to the amount of past taxes paid into the program and leave the welfare function to be performed by the SSI program. This widely advocated change, similar to the proposals of the Brookings Institution and the National Federation of Independent Business, would not reduce benefits or expenditures in general, but would make it easier for individuals to compare social security with private alternatives.

One of the current welfare elements that would be eliminated under this reform is the progressivity of the benefit formula. As we saw in chapter 2, the benefit formula is weighted so that those with lower incomes will get a higher percentage of their past taxes paid in benefits than those with higher incomes. This progressivity would be replaced by a formula strictly proportional to past taxes paid into the program. Other welfare elements which would be eliminated include the additional benefits that retired and disabled workers receive for spouses and dependents, the maximum cap on monthly benefits, and the earnings test which reduces benefits if a beneficiary earns more than a certain minimum amount in employment. Congress took a step in this direction in 1981 by eliminating the minimum monthly benefit for new beneficiaries. The elimination of these various benefits would be offset by increasing the amount of benefits that workers would receive through the strictly proportional benefit formula.

Regardless of whether these reforms are adopted, however, the reforms described below are still overwhelmingly beneficial and should be implemented.

A Quick Alternative

In an earlier work, I advanced a reform proposal designed to accomplish the necessary changes as quickly as possible.[19] We will advance

[19]Ibid., chap. 12.

below a modified version that is stretched out over more years and may be more politically salable, but this quick alternative should still be reviewed.

The first step in this reform is to abolish the payroll tax and stop the accrual of further benefit obligations and liabilities. The next step would be to calculate the age at which individuals could still receive more in the private sector than they could through social security. As individuals get older, the amount they can accumulate for retirement by beginning to save and invest outside of social security is reduced. Eventually, each will reach a point where the amount he could accumulate on his own outside of the program is less than what he could get if he continued in social security. This age is probably somewhere between 35 and 40.[20]

All individuals below this age would be required to save a certain percentage of their incomes for retirement and insurance protection in their own Individual Retirement Accounts (IRAs). These individuals could then use these funds to purchase a package of private alternatives to social security. This package would include retirement investments and life, disability, and old-age health insurance. Individuals who choose this option, however, would receive no future benefits from social security and therefore would have to rely solely on the private alternatives chosen. Though this means that these individuals would receive nothing for their past tax payments into the program, this is not unfair since these individuals should receive even higher benefits from the private alternatives than if they had been forced to stay in social security. These individuals could choose to use some of their savings at any time to buy some of the social security bonds described below and, in this case, they would receive the benefits to which those bonds entitle them in additon to any private benefits.

Alternatively, these individuals could choose to stay in social security. Those who choose this option would receive bonds which would entitle them to a proportion of future expected social security benefits

[20]Professor Feldstein calculates that all those at least under the age of 35 could still do better with an invested system than with social security, assuming a low constant real rate of return of 3 percent. Martin S. Feldstein and Anthony Pellechio, "Social Security Wealth: The Impact of Alternative Inflation Adjustments," Conference on Financing Social Security, American Enterprise Institute, 1977. In an article in 1966, Buchanan and Professor Colin Campbell of Dartmouth suggested this age would be 39. James M. Buchanan and Colin B. Campbell, "Voluntary Social Security," Wall Street Journal, December 20, 1966. The higher the assumed real rate of return individuals can earn in the private system, the higher this age will be. If the tax exemptions for retirement investments that we will propose below are instituted, the age at which individuals starting over could do at least as well in the private system as social security may be 40 or even higher.

equal to the proportion of expected lifetime taxes which they had already paid. These bonds would not be transferable nor redeemable until age 62, and they would be redeemable at that age only if the individual continues to stay in the optional social security system for the rest of his working years.

These individuals would then use their future social security taxes to purchase social security bonds from the federal government.

Part of the purchase price for these additional bonds would be for term life insurance, part for disability insurance, part for old-age health insurance, and part for retirement benefits. The bonds would then pay life insurance benefits, disability benefits, and health insurance benefits in amounts strictly related actuarially to the portion of the purchase price paid for each. In addition to these actuarial amounts, however, the government would also increase the benefits to be paid by the rate of inflation each year.

The retirement portion of each bond would increase in value each year at the rate of inflation. At retirement, the worker would receive an annuity for his bonds, which would pay him monthly benefits for the rest of his life strictly related actuarially to the accumulated value of those bonds. The monthly benefits could be adjusted so that reduced benefits could be paid for the life of a surviving spouse. The retirement benefits paid by these bonds would also be increased each year at the rate of inflation.

No interest is paid on the social security bonds under this new system because the program is operated on a pay-as-you-go basis and therefore no investments are made to earn any interest. The program can consequently only return to the individual what he has paid into it in the past. Indexing the value of the bonds to inflation only means that past payments are returned in real terms, equal to the actual value of what was paid for the bonds in the first place.

A somewhat different set of rules would apply to the workers older than this group, up to age 60. These individuals would all be given social security bonds that reach maturity upon retirement, death, or disability. At maturity, these bonds would total to an amount equal to what these individuals are currently promised in benefits under social security *minus* what they could get in the private sector if they began saving and investing now what they would otherwise pay in social security taxes.

These individuals would still be required to save the same percentage of their incomes in their IRAs as the younger workers. They would also have the option of using their funds to invest in the private alternatives. If they take this option, they will receive at least as much in benefits as they would have received under the current system. Individuals who choose to stay in social security will be required to use their mandated savings to purchase additional social security bonds structured as those described above for younger workers. Since these bonds will only return what workers paid into the system in real terms, this option will probably result in less benefits than under the current social security system. Nevertheless, since these workers could always opt for the private alternatives, they would not be made worse off by the reform (they will, in fact, be made better off in a number of ways) and therefore should not oppose it.

For all those over age 60, the government would continue to pay them what they are currently promised in social security benefits. As new workers entered the system, they would have the option of using their saved IRA funds to purchase the private alternatives or the described social security bonds. Remaining social security benefit obligations would be financed from general revenues.

Since the private alternatives under this reform proposal are superior to social security for all those below age 60, virtually all individuals below this age should opt for these alternatives. Over time, therefore, the amount of necessary general revenue financing will decline as more and more individuals retire with a larger and larger portion of their retirement benefits paid through private alternatives. Eventually, all those in the older age group of workers at the time the reform was instituted will have died, and virtually all those who were in the younger group, as well as new, young workers, will be relying primarily on private alternatives. At this point, the need for general revenue funds to finance benefits would be eliminated. Those who were still in the program for whatever reason would be paying for their own benefits directly through the purchase of social security bonds, assuming that the government could maintain the value in real terms of the money it is given for these bonds.

At the same time that remaining social security benefit obligations decrease due to these factors, general revenues to finance them will be increasing as a result of our reform. The increased savings and investment through IRAs will be generating new income which will be partially taxed through the corporate income tax.[21] The increased wages

---

[21]Though dividends paid into IRAs are tax-exempt, the corporation must pay the corporate income tax before it can pay these dividends. Consequently, even with current IRA tax exemptions, investments through IRAs are partially taxed. This taxation continues because IRAs currently only eliminate one branch of the double taxation of corporate income.

and new employment resulting from this investment will result in increases in individual income tax revenues. The discouraging effects of the payroll tax will be eliminated, leading to further increases in employment, GNP, and hence, tax revenues.[22] The new investment will also have a stimulative ripple effect throughout the economy, leading to further increases in tax revenues.

Eventually, these increasing tax revenues will reach and then surpass the amount of general revenues necessary to finance the declining social security benefit obligations. Long before these remaining obligations are completely phased out, therefore, the reform will, in effect, become completely self-financing, with no general revenues needed that are not naturally generated as part of the reform.

Once the necessary net general revenue subsidies are reduced to a tolerable level, due to trends of reduced expenditures and increased revenues, an expanded system of tax exemptions for IRA investments should be phased in. This system would allow individuals to receive the full, before-tax, rate of return on their IRA investments. The proposed changes will be described in detail in the next section. Also, after the reform is fully phased in, the requirement that individuals save a certain percentage of their incomes could be phased out. As individuals become familiar with the new system, this paternalistic requirement may no longer be necessary.

The welfare function of the current social security system would be served under this proposed reform through the SSI program, which, as we discussed in chapter 2, provides means-tested welfare benefits financed out of general revenues for the elderly and disabled poor. Individuals needing the welfare benefits previously supplied by social security would automatically qualify for benefits under the means-tested SSI program. This program could be updated to ensure that it could adequately perform this role.

The costs of this reform are the necessary annual general revenue expenditures needed to pay continuing social security benefit obligations. While these costs are only transitory and would eventually be eliminated entirely, they would be substantial in the early years. Even

---

[22] As we saw in chapter 3, because social security benefits are so unrelated to past payments into the program, workers tend to view these payments as a tax, which reduces their compensation for working and therefore discourages employment. As a result of our reform, however, workers will be paying these monies into the private system rather than into social security. Since benefits paid under the private system are directly related to these past payments, workers will tend to view these payments as part of their compensation, which they are in effect banking away. Our reform should therefore eliminate these discouraging effects of the payroll tax.

assuming the reform initially applied only to the OASDI portion of social security, if begun in calendar year 1982, it would require a general revenue subsidy of $146 billion in that year. This would of course decline in the years immediately following due to reduced benefit expenditures and increased tax revenues, probably falling to minor levels in a decade or less.[23] Nevertheless, the amounts needed in the initial years, as with many of the reforms noted above, may be too large for the federal government to meet without unacceptably high tax increases, or borrowing requirements, or politically infeasible expenditure reductions. This is, however, the only major drawback. If ways could be found to meet the initial general revenue requirements without great pain, this reform would be ideal.

A Measured Alternative

A revamped version of this reform can avoid this problem, however, and provide a number of additional benefits. This reform builds on the provision in the 1981 tax act that extended the availability of IRAs to all workers. The first step in the revamped reform would be to allow individuals to deduct their annual contributions to these IRAs from their payroll taxes for the OASI portion of the program, up to an annual maximum of 50 percent of such taxes. Individuals could also direct their employers to contribute up to 50 percent of the employer share of the OASI tax to their IRAs, with the employers deducting these contributions from their social security taxes as well.

The second step is to reduce the future OASI benefits of individuals to the extent that each took advantage of this option. For example, if an individual deducted IRA contributions equal to the maximum of 50 percent of his OASI taxes all of his working life, his future OASI benefits would be reduced by 50 percent. If he deducted contributions equal to 50 percent of such taxes for half of his life, his future benefits would be reduced by 25 percent. If he deducted amounts equal to 15 percent of his taxes for one-third of his working life, his future benefits would be reduced by 5 percent.

Each individual, however, would have the benefits payable from his accumulated IRA funds to make up for this loss. The combination of these private-sector benefits and the remaining OASI benefits should be greater than currently expected OASI benefits alone since, as we have discussed, benefits payable through private alternatives to social security should be higher. At the time of the reform, individuals should

[23]See Ferrara, *Social Security: The Inherent Contradiction*, chap. 12.

108

be allowed to purchase life insurance through their IRAs so that they could replace any lost survivors insurance benefits.

These changes would in effect allow individuals to use part of their social security taxes to purchase private alternatives to social security, with those alternatives eventually replacing part of the program. It is true that today individuals can already deduct their contributions for IRAs from their income in computing their federal income tax. But this merely means that the portion of income that each individual sets aside for retirement is untaxed. To allow individuals to use their social security taxes to purchase private alternatives, the IRA contributions must also be deductible from social security taxes.

After these changes, the government would continue to pay the otherwise promised social security benefits, making up for the lost payroll taxes out of general revenues. Over time, however, this general revenue subsidy would decline, and eventually be eliminated, due to the same two factors reducing the net subsidy under the alternative discussed above. First, more and more individuals would be retiring with a larger portion of their retirement benefits from private alternatives, reducing the amount of social security benefit expenditures. Second, the increased investment through IRAs would result in increased general revenues through the corporate income tax and other taxes, increasing the tax resources available to pay the continuing social security expenditures.

As the net subsidy shrank or as the budget otherwise allowed, the percentage of OASI taxes against which IRA contributions could be deducted could be increased from 50 percent to 100 percent. (At each step in the reform, of course, the maximum amount each individual could contribute to his IRA would have to be at least equal to the maximum amount which he and his employer could deduct from their social security taxes.) Individuals would then have their OASI benefits reduced to the extent they took advantage of this option, with their IRA funds to make up the difference. An individual who deducted contributions equal to 100 percent of his OASI taxes all of his working life would receive no OASI benefits, but would have his accumulated IRA funds instead.

Of course the government would continue to finance current OASI benefit obligations, using general revenues as necessary. When the necessary general revenue subsidies were again reduced to minor levels due to the factors noted above, individuals could then deduct IRA contributions against 100 percent of DI and HI taxes as well. DI and HI benefits would then also be reduced to the extent individuals took advantage of this option, and the government would continue to finance remaining benefits out of general revenues. Individuals at this point would also have to be allowed to buy private disability insurance and old-age health insurance through their IRAs to replace the lost benefits.

After this point, the same two factors discussed above would continue to work to eliminate the remaining necessary general revenue subsidy. Once this is achieved, the insurance portion of the program will have become completely privatized. The welfare portion of the program would again be automatically picked up by the SSI program as under the quick alternative reform described above. It should be reiterated that the SSI program could be restructured as part of this reform to ensure that it could perform this function adequately. The end result of the reform would thus be that the welfare and insurance functions of the current social security program would be separated into two entirely different sets of institutions, with the insurance function completely privatized.

The final element of this reform, after the other elements had been phased in, would be to enact further tax exemptions for the IRA accounts so that individuals would receive the full, before-tax, rate of return on their IRA investments. Currently, as we have noted, the portion of income saved in IRAs is tax deductible in computing federal income tax. In addition, any dividends paid on stock or any interest paid on mortgages, bonds, or notes held in an IRA would be untaxed, as would any capital gains made from the sale of assets held by these accounts. Benefits payable out of IRAs, however, are taxable at the regular income tax rate of the recipient at that time.

A further tax exemption is needed, however, to eliminate both branches of the double taxation of corporate income for IRA investments. This would involve making the profits of any corporation tax-exempt to the extent its stock was held by IRAs. A corporation with half of its stock held by these accounts would have half its income tax-exempt; a corporation wholly owned by IRA accounts would be entirely tax-exempt. To ensure that the IRAs received the full benefit of this tax exemption, their availability to corporations would be made contingent on distribution of the full tax savings to the accounts in the form of cash dividends.

The same tax treatment should apply to debt securities held by IRAs. If an account lends money to a corporation and the corporation has to pay half of whatever it earns with that money in taxes, the corporation will not be willing to pay as high an interest rate for that money as it would if it did not have to pay any taxes. The corporation should

110

therefore be tax-exempt on whatever it earns with money borrowed from an IRA. As corporations bid for IRA loans, the interest rates they have to pay would rise so that the accounts would ultimately receive the full benefit of the tax exemption. Generally, then, a corporation should be tax-exempt to the extent that it derived any of its assets, whether through debt or equity, from IRA accounts.

This general rule should also apply to noncorporate businesses or ventures. An apartment building half-owned by IRAs should have half its net income from rents tax-exempt. A business partnership with three-quarters of its capital held by IRAs in either debt or equity form should be three-quarters tax-exempt. Such noncorporate entities would be automatically tax-exempt to the extent that they were owned by IRAs as long as IRAs were legally allowed to own them. A noncorporate partnership would have its income attributed to its various partners for tax purposes according to the percentage of the business each partner owned (the amount of equity capital each partner had contributed). Those partners who did not invest in the business through retirement accounts would be fully taxed in the usual way. Those partners who did invest in the business through such accounts would simply be tax-exempt on the portion of the partnership income attributable to them. Any restrictions on the ownership of these entities by IRAs could be eased as part of our reform. Non-corporate entities in general could then also be made tax-exempt to the extent that they borrowed funds from IRAs. This tax exemption would accrue to the accounts through higher interest rates on their loans.

Another tax change would be to make the purchase of life, disability, and old-age health insurance policies through IRAs tax-exempt. This would involve making the returns to insurance companies from the sale of such policies exempt from tax. Investments made by insurance companies to support these policies also would be free from tax, just as the investments made directly through IRAs. Corporations or other businesses that obtained equity or debt capital from such investments would be proportionally tax-exempt, as discussed above. The effect of these tax changes would be to lower the insurance premiums on policies purchased through IRAs, reflecting the full, real, before-tax return that would be accruing to the supporting investments.

The final tax change would be to make the benefits payable through IRAs at retirement or otherwise also tax-exempt. This would simply treat the private system the same as social security, since the program's benefits are currently untaxed. Another tax element of the new system, which is technically not a change because no directly analogous element currently exists, is that individuals would not be allowed to deduct from their income in computing their federal income tax amounts that are paid into their IRAs by their employers. The employer's share of the social security tax is not currently included in the employee's gross income, so there is no reason to allow a deduction against this income if the employer is allowed to pay these funds into the employee's IRA instead.

If the amount that each individual could contribute to his IRA each year is limited to the amount he would have paid in social security taxes, including both the employer and employee shares, these new tax exemptions should not result in a substantial loss of federal revenues. This is because these provisions would merely exempt from taxation the additional production created by the investment of social security taxes. This production is not being taxed now because social security taxes are not being invested now and, therefore, this production is not now even being created. The tax exemption of retirement benefits under the new system could not result in any revenue loss since social security benefits, which these private retirement benefits replace, are not taxed now either. The retirement benefits under the new system exceeding what social security benefits would have been simply represent income that is not being produced now and is therefore also not taxed. Finally, the exemption of the portion of each individual's ordinary income which he saves in his retirement account would be no different than under the current IRA system.[24]

These new tax rules would simply allow investors to receive the full value of the extra production produced by their retirement investments—the full, before-tax rate of return on capital investment esti-

[24]The only significant loss of federal revenue from the new IRA system would result from the fact that individuals would have invested some funds in presently existing IRAs without these changes. Under the present system, the investment of these funds would have generated some additional tax revenue through the corporate income tax. But under the new system, this taxation would be abolished, and consequently these revenues would be lost.

If individuals could substitute IRA savings for other savings, then the replacement of these taxed savings with tax-free IRA funds would result in the loss of further revenues. But since IRA funds could not be used until retirement, except for insurance contingencies, they are not substitutable for other savings.

The amount under the new system that each individual could deduct from his ordinary income due to IRA savings would be equal to the employee share of the social security tax, which is roughly the same as under current law, so no new revenue loss would result on this account. An additional minor loss might result to the extent that individuals increased their IRA savings over what they would have saved under the present system, and therefore increase their deduction against ordinary incomes.

112

mated by economists at 12 percent or more.[25] Of course, with this rate of return individuals would receive even greater benefits through the private retirement system than we saw in chapter 4. Since people are using these funds to provide for their retirement and critical insurance contingencies, this new, expanded system of IRA tax exemptions should clearly be adopted. The government should not be seizing and forcibly reallocating to other uses the assets individuals have set aside for these important ends. The full retirement benefits that individuals would receive under this new system would not in any way constitute a burden to society, and, in fact, would be entirely earned, since these benefits would be financed entirely from the increased production resulting from the investments of each individual for his retirement. This tax exemption system would simply remove all the barriers that the government is currently placing in the way of individuals trying to achieve retirement security.

While this new system for tax exemptions might appear complex at first glance, it is actually relatively simple and straightforward compared to the many other types of special exemptions in the tax code. The new system is simply a modified version of the IRA that is already provided for in the current tax code. The only new issue raised by the new system is to what extent a particular business venture was financed with funds from IRAs. This could be easily resolved by reference to the ordinary records of financial transactions. This would be one of the simplest issues presented by the tax code. It would be far easier than the issues presented by the rules for recaptured depreciation, the sale and lease-back of certain properties, or the taxation of corporate reorganizations. The new system of IRA tax exemptions could, in fact, greatly simplify the tax code because it could replace the many varying types of special exemptions for different types of retirement and pension plans now in the code.

How It Would Work

The adoption of this reform would lead to the establishment of an entirely new framework, which would cover all of the contingencies covered by our current social security system. Its key characteristic would be a reliance on voluntary, cooperative, decentralized, market institutions, instead of centralized, bureaucratic, coercive, government institutions.

The retirement insurance function of the current system would be covered by each individual saving in his own IRA the money he would

[25]See discussion in chap. 4.

113

otherwise pay in social security taxes. The money in this retirement account could then be invested in numerous economically productive private investment alternatives, which would earn a rate of return that would allow the account to pay much greater retirement benefits than social security. The individual could make these investments on his own or they could be made on his behalf by banks, insurance companies, trust companies, pension plan managers and other market institutions which have the information and expertise to make such investments wisely.

Once an individual has reached retirement, he will have accumulated a large sum in his retirement account that could then be used to finance his retirement benefits. The individual could simply use the interest on the fund and leave the fund itself to his children, or use the fund to purchase an annuity contract, which would guarantee him a certain income for the rest of his life. The annuity could be adjusted to continue payments for the life of any surviving spouse. The individual could also keep the fund and vary the amount of income he would draw from it over his retirement years. He could use some of the money in the account to give lifetime gifts or as a special reserve in case of emergencies. Each individual would in fact have complete control over the money to spend as he wished. In addition, he would not lose the money through any disqualifying act, such as marriage, divorce, or work, as can happen now under social security. Thus, his life would be freer from government restrictions.

An important feature of this new retirement system is that it would provide instantaneous vesting and portability rights. Once the individual puts the money in his IRA, the future benefits that money could support would be his, regardless of any future actions, such as switching jobs. Moreover, the money saved in his IRA would follow him wherever he might roam.

The survivors insurance function of the current social security system would also be served through these IRAs. Survivors insurance is nothing more than term life insurance. Each individual can use some of the money he or she would have paid in social security taxes to purchase term life insurance through his IRA from private insurance companies. If the individual dies before his retirement, he can leave his spouse and children both the life insurance amount and the saved amount for retirement in his IRA. These funds could then be used to finance the benefits to replace the survivors benefits social security would have paid.

An individual, therefore, only needs to purchase a life insurance policy in an amount equal to the amount of desired insurance protec-

114

tion, minus the amount in his retirement account. As his retirement account grows, the amount of term life insurance he needs to buy will decline. This amount will reach zero when his retirement account is greater than the desired amount of survivors protection. If the desired amount of survivors protection is the same as is currently provided by social security, then for most individuals the fund alone will be enough to provide these benefits without the purchase of additional term life insurance some time between the ages of 40 and 45. This assumes that the individual enters the work force now, at the beginning of his working life and invests in his IRA all that he would have paid in social security taxes under the current system.[26] After this age, our new system would pay more in survivors benefits for workers than the current social security system.

Thus, if the individual dies before retirement, through these private alternatives he can leave his family an amount equal to or greater than what social security would provide. Furthermore, this private arrangement will be far superior to social security because the family will be left in complete control of the assets, which they can use in any way they desire for the rest of their lives, with no disqualifications. In addition, if the worker is not married and has no dependents, he need not purchase life insurance through his IRA, as social security requires him to do. He can instead save more for his retirement. But if he does purchase such insurance, the amount purchased will still be left for his heirs along with his retirement account, unlike social security.

Individuals can similarly purchase disability insurance through their IRAs from private insurance companies, with some of the money they would otherwise pay into social security. They can also use some of the money in their retirement accounts for support in the event of disability. As the fund grows, the individual can again decrease the amount of disability insurance he is purchasing so that the amount of insurance plus the amount in his fund will be enough at any time to pay him all the benefits social security would have paid him in the event of disability, including retirement benefits. The amount of disability insurance purchased under this arrangement would again fall to zero for workers currently entering the work force some time in their forties, assuming again that they invested all that they would have otherwise paid in social security taxes in their IRAs.[27]

Old-age health insurance could also be covered by IRAs. Each individual can use some of the money he would have paid into social

[26]See Ferrara, *Social Security: The Inherent Contradiction*, chap. 4.
[27]Ibid.

security to purchase old-age health insurance from private insurance companies through his IRA. If workers signed up for such policies early in life, even though coverage would not begin until after retirement, they could pay a very small premium each month. The insurance company would use these premiums to fund future benefits by making investments; the income from these investments would allow the premiums to be even lower. Another advantage of early purchase is that individuals early in life present relatively equal risks of being in poor health in retirement; therefore the problem of being unable to obtain health insurance in old age could be avoided. Individuals could purchase this insurance when they start work as part of an overall package of life, disability, health, and retirement insurance.

The other function performed by the current social security system is the welfare function. As we saw in chapter 3, those individuals who do work regularly, even at low wages, should be able to receive adequate retirement benefits under the new system by using the money they are now paying in social security taxes to invest in private alternatives. But individuals who are not regularly employed do not now pay substantial social security taxes, and therefore could not obtain adequate benefits through the use of these funds in the private system. These individuals simply do not have sufficient funds to save for an adequate retirement or provide for insurance contingencies. Through its welfare function, social security now seeks to provide these individuals with the necessary retirement and insurance benefits, even though these benefits have not been paid for or earned.

Under our reform, this function, as we have noted, would be immediately assumed by the government through the SSI program, updated to ensure that it could adequately perform this role. Since the SSI program utilizes a means test, providing the necessary welfare benefits through this mechanism would ensure that benefits are paid only to those in need, unlike social security, which wastes welfare benefits on those who are not poor. These benefits would be financed by the progressive general revenue tax system, unlike social security, which finances its benefits counterproductively through the regressive payroll tax. At the same time, the poor would be ensured adequate benefit levels. This means of providing welfare benefits could later be revamped as part of a general program of welfare reform.

The new system could be structured to include a major role for private charities. An expanded system of tax credits for charitable contributions could make such private institutions even more viable. But the ideal welfare system is a topic for another book.

The new system emerging from our reform proposal would in effect require that each individual save at least as much for his retirement and insurance contingencies as he would otherwise be required to pay in social security taxes. Individuals must either annually invest such sums in their IRAs or continue to pay them into social security. This feature should eliminate any fear that without social security, individuals will simply not save or provide for their retirement or major, insurable dangers.

Because of the much higher benefits that could be provided by the private alternatives, this requirement should at least be lowered eventually. The amount of benefits which could be purchased through the private system by using all the money that would otherwise be paid in social security taxes is probably higher than that for which most individuals would want to pay. In any event, this amount is more than should be mandated through a savings requirement. At best, only a minimum floor of benefits necessary to keep people out of poverty should be required. Reducing the savings requirement would increase the discretionary, take-home pay of working people above what they would have under the current social security system, if they chose to save less than the amount they would otherwise have had to pay in social security taxes.

Any such savings requirement could also be structured with some degree of flexibility. Individuals might be allowed to save less than the minimum during some periods if they saved more during other periods. This would allow, for example, young couples buying their first home to reduce their retirement savings and increase them later when their income increases.

Ideally, there should be no savings requirement at all, as was discussed in chapter 9. The paternalistic rationale underlying such a requirement would not be a sufficient justification in a truly free and liberal society. This requirement should therefore be phased out completely after individuals become comfortable with the new system. But given the current state of public opinion, it is probably not possible to reform social security as we have proposed without some initial savings requirement.

Our new system also retains an option to stay in social security as it currently is structured. After our reform is completely phased in, however, this remaining, optional, social security system should be reformed. The current system of benefits should be replaced with the system of social security bonds as described above under the quick alternative reform above. Those remaining in the social security system would receive bonds for their past tax payments which would entitle them to a proportion of future expected benefits equal to the proportion of expected lifetime taxes represented by these past payments. Those who wanted to remain in social security would thereafter purchase additional social security bonds which would pay actuarially determined, but inflation-adjusted, retirement, survivor, disability, and old-age health benefits, as described above.

This would make the benefits of the remaining social security system strictly proportional to taxes paid into the system, eliminating the welfare elements. The private alternative system, however, would be superior to social security either as it is currently structured or reformed into the social security bond system. Most, if not all, individuals could therefore be expected to opt for the private alternatives in either case.

Reforming the remaining, optional social security system into a system built on bonds with strictly proportional benefits would be attractive from a public-policy viewpoint, if it were politically viable. If the current system continued unchanged as an option, taxpayers would be subsidizing its benefits. Since the money paid into this system would not be invested, but immediately paid out on a pay-as-you-go basis, this money would not earn any return and the system would not have sufficient funds to pay the promised benefits above the value of what was paid into the system in real terms. The payment of these benefits might require continued general revenue subsidies to the remaining, optimal social security system even after our reform is fully phased in.[28] The subsidization of these benefits by taxpayers would create an unfair bias against the private options, although these options would still be superior as long as the social security bond benefit levels were not subsidized to heights beyond currently expected social security benefit levels.

The reformed bond system would eliminate this subsidy. Individuals under this system would receive back in benefits only what they paid into it in real terms. This would eliminate any bias against the private

[28]If the percentage of the population that chose to remain in social security was stable, and if the amount of promised social security benefits was no greater than those that would be paid through the pay-as-you-go "social security rate of return" (rate of growth in wages plus rate of growth in population), then continuing payments into the program alone would be enough to pay continuing benefit obligations once our reform was entirely phased in. (Such benefits could still be considered subsidized, however, since any returns above the real value of what was paid in would not have been earned, as the social security payments themselves would not have resulted in increased production to finance those returns.) If the percentage opting for social security were falling, or if benefits were greater than noted above, then the continuing benefit obligations of the optional social security system would have to be general-revenue subsidized.

option and any opportunity for continued general revenue subsidies for social security. It would make the costs and benefits of continuing in this optional system clear to those who chose to participate, and they would bear both fully. It would eliminate any continuing inequities within the optional system itself.

Moreover, reforming the remaining social security option along these lines would eliminate the need for a Social Security Administration. The bonds could be sold by the Treasury Department, and they could be named to avoid any reference to social security. This would make subsidizing the bonds more blatant and awkward, and minimize the chance that the old program would in effect be resurrected through such subsidies. It would also eliminate a bureaucracy that might have an interest in reversing fundamental reform.

But these changes on the remaining social security option aren't essential to our reform. The reform would still be well worthwhile even if these changes could not be included for political reasons.

The private, alternative system resulting from our reform would also contain a mechanism that would in effect index benefits to increase at the rate of inflation. As prices increase with inflation, the value of the assets that individuals hold in their IRAs would, on the average, increase at the same rate over the long run. The prices charged for the goods and services produced by these IRA investments will also, on the average, increase at the rate of inflation. The profit or rate of return on these investments will therefore increase with inflation as well.

While an individual is working and accumulating his retirement fund, therefore, the future benefits that this fund would be able to pay would be increasing at the rate of inflation because of this automatic adjustment process. If an individual chooses to live off the interest on this fund in retirement, his benefits will continue to increase at the rate of inflation because of this process. Similarly, if an individual purchases an annuity, it should be possible for the seller of the annuity to agree to pay benefits in real terms, adjusted for inflation, because of this automatic adjustment process in the investments that would support the annuity. The same is true for benefits paid under life, disability, and health insurance policies. Thus, individuals in the private, alternative system should be able to maintain their expected benefits in real terms regardless of inflation.

In chapter 4, we saw the benefits individuals could expect to receive from their IRA investments. These benefits were presented in real terms, adjusted for inflation, so their apparent value will not be depreciated by inflation in any way. These benefits were, of course, still much higher than those which could be paid through social security in real, inflation-adjusted terms. The process described here indicates why the private system can maintain these benefits in real terms.

This mechanism should be sufficient to guard the private system of benefits against inflation. But if politically it appeared that further efforts were necessary, the government could guarantee private benefits against inflation under a system similar to that advanced by A. Haeworth Robertson, as discussed earlier. Under this system, the government would supplement the benefits that could be paid out of private IRAs with regular, general revenue-financed payments, which would increase these benefits each year at the rate of inflation. These supplemental benefits would amount to an unnecessary, unearned supplemental grant of welfare to virtually everybody. Nevertheless, such supplementation should completely eliminate any special concerns about the protection of benefits against inflation under the private system. If such a feature were necessary to win legislative approval of the reform, it would be well worth including in the overall reform package.

Finally, the new system resulting from our reform would contain many options for those who wanted some form of government guarantee of their retirement investments. Individuals could, for example, invest through their IRAs in vehicles that were already guaranteed by the government. These would include Treasury Bills, state and local government bonds, and deposits at banks and savings and loans. Individuals could be allowed to use their IRA funds to invest in pension plans guaranteed by the Federal Pension Benefit Guarantee Corporation. In addition, individuals could choose the remaining social security option for government-guaranteed benefits.

Any further government guarantees should be unnecessary. Individuals should be free to choose their own IRA investments from the wide range of alternatives available in the market. Those who wished to obtain the higher returns associated with riskier investments should be free to do so. If they were successful, under our system of IRA tax exemptions they would receive the full benefits. But if some of their investments fail, they should bear the loss. Many private investment options exist which would pay substantial returns and would be quite safe for prudent, long-term IRA investments. Though they would not have government guarantees, they would be quite unlikely to fail completely. These include such options as money-market funds and a diversified portfolio of common stock. An individual's IRA investments could always include some of the government-guaranteed investments for safety. Ultimately, an individual who failed completely would be protected from poverty by the continuing government welfare program, which is part of our new, reformed system.

The Costs and the Benefits

Our proposed reform would not entail any increase in government expenditures. The reform would instead steadily reduce federal expenditures over many years. But the reform would require annual general-revenue subsidies of the social security program for a number of years to replace payroll tax revenues lost due to the deductibility of IRA contributions against payroll tax liability. These annual general-revenue subsidies can be thought of as the cost of the program.

If calendar year 1982 were the first year of the reform, and all workers took full advantage of the opportunity to deduct their IRA contributions against up to 50 percent of their OASI tax liability, a general-revenue subsidy to social security of $62 billion would be necessary in that year.[29] The amount of this necessary subsidy would, on net, decline in future years due to the two factors discussed earlier. If the second stage of the reform, allowing deductibility against 100 percent of OASI taxes, were implemented after four years, the necessary general-revenue subsidy would increase by an amount equivalent, in relation to the budget and the economy of that year, to the $62-billion-dollar subsidy needed in 1982.[30] The necessary subsidy would then resume its decline until the third stage of the reform could be implemented, allowing deductions against 100 percent of the DI and HI tax. If this occurred after another four years had passed, the necessary general-revenue subsidy would increase by the equivalent of $57 billion in 1982.[31] Thus, if this reform schedule were adopted, individuals would be able to start substituting the private alternatives for the entire OASI portion of the program after four years, and for the entire program after eight years.

While it would admittedly be difficult to begin this reform in the midst of the current budgetary problems, in normal times these should be feasible amounts for the federal government to absorb. As noted earlier, the general revenues to finance these subsidies should not come from an increase in tax rates, nor from borrowing. Instead, the federal revenue increases which naturally occur over time as a result of eco-

[29]Social Security Board of Trustees, *1982 Annual Report of the Board of Trustees of the Federal Old-Age and Survivors Insurance and Disability Insurance Trust Fund.*
[30]Ibid, p. 54.
[31]Social Security Board of Trustees, *1982 Annual Report of the Board of Trustees of the Federal Hospital Insurance Trust Fund,* p. 29.

nomic growth should be used, instead of using these revenues for other new programs. After this, additional revenues could be made available by restraining the growth of other government expenditures, or by cutting back on some programs. Further revenue could be raised by selling off certain government assets. Since eliminating the unfunded social security liability is a one-time, transitory expense, this is an appropriate way to finance the reform. The American Society of Appraisers estimates that the value of *surplus* federal land holdings, not land deliberately held out of use, amounts to $100 billion.[32] Further help in meeting the necessary general-revenue subsidies could be obtained by adopting some of the preliminary reforms noted earlier. Switching from the current wage indexing system to indexing to the lower of wages or prices, as well as delaying the retirement age from 65 to 68, would substantially reduce the benefit expenditures that need to be general-revenue financed, particularly in the later years of the reform.

Of course, the reform could be phased in more slowly and over more years. If IRA contributions were initially deductible against only 35 percent of OASI taxes, then the necessary subsidy in the first year would be at most $44 billion. If the maximum percentage were initially 20 percent, then the maximum subsidy in the first year would be $25 billion.

For some individuals, conceptually it may be useful to think of our proposed social security reform as a new government program, with the necessary, transitory general-revenue subsidies as the cost of the program. Or it may be useful to think of the reform as a new tax cut, which it really is, with the necessary, transitory subsidies representing the loss in revenues. We will undoubtedly enact new programs or new tax cuts approaching this magnitude some time in the future. Our proposed social security reform should be considered as one of the alternatives among these new programs or tax cuts. If the reform does indeed appear to be far more beneficial than any of the other options, as is suggested below, then it should be implemented at the earliest possible time, delaying the other alternatives.

The cost of our proposed reform should be viewed in perspective. The reform eliminates an unfunded social security liability of almost $6 trillion. It privatizes the functions of a program accounting for over one-fourth of the entire federal government. The necessary transitory, general-revenue subsidies are quite modest amounts to pay to achieve

[32]As reported by Dexter MacBride, American Society of Appraisers, March 1982.

such ends. Indeed, these subsidy amounts are a bargain since they would allow taxpayers to avoid the huge future tax increases that will be necessary to fund the program as currently structured.

The beneficial effects of the reform that can be bought for this cost are truly overwhelming. To begin with, the reform would have several extremely beneficial effects on the economy. There would be an enormous increase in the savings and capital supply as individuals saved and invested the money they are currently paying in social security taxes. With the reform fully phased in, this increase would amount to hundreds of billions of dollars annually, eventually increasing the total savings and capital supply by 40 percent.

This increase would result in new capital investment that would modernize our factories, improving their efficiency and making them competitive with foreign producers. It would provide more money for mortgages, thereby increasing the current housing supply. It would provide the necessary funds to search out, discover, and develop new energy supplies. It would create a large number of new jobs, lowering unemployment. This new capital investment would also increase wages, which would upgrade existing jobs, thereby creating more good jobs.

Fundamentally, this increase in savings and capital investment would eventually result in a sharp increase in GNP. If this reform had been fully implemented in today's economy, the GNP would have been higher by approximately $550 billion, or $2,400 per person and $6,600 per family. Moreover, without the discouraging effects of the payroll tax and the earnings test, employment would grow, increasing national income even further. The special skills and experience of the elderly would again be brought into productive use, instead of wasting away in idleness imposed by social security restrictions.

Perhaps the most important benefit of the reform is that young people entering the work force today would be able to receive far higher benefits than they would otherwise have received through social security. They would be able to accumulate enormous trust funds in their IRAs by their retirement years and the benefits financed by these funds would be much greater than those that social security would pay. Even for average families, these funds could climb to well over a half million in today's dollars. Workers with higher incomes could accumulate funds of $1 million or more by retirement.

These young people would also each be able to buy a personally tailored package of insurance and investment plans that is suited to their individual needs and preferences. Through their IRAs, they could each put together such a package from the wide variety of options available in the market place. They would also no longer be required to pay for insurance protection that they do not need. Single people, for example, would not be forced to purchase term life insurance, particularly in a form in which they could never collect, as with social security.

Furthermore, the money individuals save and invest under the new system would be under their complete personal control once retirement is reached, and they could then use and spend these funds as they desire. Moreover, they would not be subject to the possible loss of these funds due to any disqualifying act, such as work or marriage, as can happen under social security. They would therefore no longer be subject to government restrictions over their personal lives just to be able to get their own money back. Indeed, under the new system individuals would have a legally enforceable right to their benefits which could not be revoked, unlike social security.

Individuals could count on the new system to deal with each of them in a fair and equitable manner, with benefits received strictly proportional to past payments made into the system. The many inequities in the current social security benefit structure would be eliminated. Moreover, individuals under the new system would be able to participate in a private retirement plan with instantaneous probability and vesting.

Another advantage of the reform is that it would solve both the short-term and long-term financing problems of the program. The projected short-term deficits of the program would in effect be met by part of the general-revenue subsidies necessary to implement the reform. This problem would therefore be solved precisely as liberals advocate. But the long-term financing problem would be solved, and solved permanently, through privatizing the insurance aspect of the program. In general, in the fully-funded private system, there would always be enough funds on hand to pay for all accrued benefit obligations. Benefits under this system would therefore no longer be vulnerable to short-term economic instabilities, demographic trends, or political whims.

The poor and members of minority groups would also greatly benefit from the reform. The improved economic performance that would result from these changes would benefit the poor the most since it is they who most need this improvement. The reduced unemployment, the increase in wages and in the availability of good jobs, the increased supplies of housing, energy, and other goods and services making up the national income all would be most meaningful and beneficial to the most needy. The poor and those with below-average incomes are also in greater need of the higher benefits available through the private,

124

invested system. These higher benefits would enable them to secure decent and adequate retirement incomes.

The discrimination against the poor in the current system, discussed in chapter 6, would also be eliminated because they would be able to buy insurance and retirement protection that is more suited to their particular needs and circumstances. The oppressive payroll tax which now bears most harshly on the poor will also have been eliminated. Welfare benefits would no longer be financed by this regressive, counterproductive tax. Welfare benefits available to help the poor would also no longer be wasted by being paid to those who are not poor. Instead, these benefits would be paid solely through the means-tested SSI program.

Minority groups would especially benefit from the flexibility in the private system for each individual to tailor his package of retirement and insurance investments to his own preferences and situation. Members of these groups, and those who follow non-traditional lifestyles, would be able to purchase the retirement and insurance protection best suited to their own special circumstances. Our reform would thus end the discrimination against these individuals prevalent in the current social security system.

Our reformed system would also no longer be subject to the political instabilities and difficulties associated with the current government program. Politicians would no longer be able to abuse the system for their own gain at the expense of the public. Politically powerful special-interest groups would no longer be able to seek special privileges for personal or ideological gain. The new private insurance system would not be subject to corrupting political influences. Individuals would no longer have to use cumbersome political channels to get the kind of protection and changes they want. They could simply arrange or rearrange their own financial affairs as they wish, and choose or switch to the plan of coverage they want from the diverse options offered in the marketplace by companies with an incentive to keep their products up-to-date with the latest trends. Each individual's personal affairs would no longer be political issues whose final resolution is in the hands of the government. Individuals would no longer have to institute national political campaigns to deal with their retirement and insurance concerns.

Our reform would also eliminate many of the coercive aspects of the current social security program. While individuals would still in effect be required to make some provision for their retirement and insurance contingencies, they would be free to make this provision through private alternatives to social security of their own choosing. Americans would therefore have greater freedom to control their own lives and incomes. Eventually, even the forced savings requirement could be phased out.

The reform would also result in a more widespread ownership of America's business and industry and a significantly broadened distribution of national wealth. Every individual would be accumulating a large retirement trust fund, which would represent his ownership interest in the country's productive assets. Adding these large, relatively equal funds held by each individual to the nation's wealth stock would result in a substantial decrease in the concentration of this wealth. As we have noted, it has been estimated that if individuals saved and invested in private IRAs all that they currently pay in social security taxes, over 40 percent of the nation's wealth would be held in this widely distributed form, and the nation's concentration of wealth would be reduced by at least one-third.[33]

The reform would thus be a way for average workers to capture a large portion of the profits of the nation's private enterprises and to use these profits to support their retirement. More fundamentally, the reform would also legitimately provide the average person with a greater voice in corporate decision-making. The workers would have at last substantially bought in as capitalists themselves, and they would have as strong and as legitimate a say in controlling the nation's enterprises as any owner should have. In addition, with a large portion of the country's business sector owned by the common man, unnecessary government regulation and oppressive business taxation are more likely to be eliminated. There would also be less opportunity for political demagogues to manipulate anti-business sentiment. The end result is likely to be a more efficient and fair overall economy.

Over the long run, our reform would also permanently cut total federal spending by more than one-fourth, with total non-defense spending decreased by more than one-half.[34] These spending reductions result from shifting the insurance functions of the current system to the private sector and by eliminating the unnecessary payment of

[33]See discussion in chap. 6.

[34]Social Security expenditures are currently well over one-fourth of the total federal budget, and this percentage will only increase in future years. By 1995, the program is projected to account for 59 percent of the total non-defense budget, excluding interest on the national debt. Statement by David A. Stockman before the Social Security Subcommittee, House Ways and Means Committee, May 28, 1981; Richard Kuzmacks, Office of Management and Budget.

welfare benefits to those who are not poor or in need. If we are to make any substantial, permanent progress in our efforts to cut federal spending, this reform is essential.

Furthermore, our reform in effect would denationalize a large portion of the insurance industry. There is no reason why the portion of the insurance industry represented by social security should remain socialized in our otherwise free-market American economy.

Finally, to top it all off, all of this would have been accomplished without raising social security taxes or cutting social security benefits. At no point in our reform are total benefits cut below what an individual can expect to receive from the current system. In fact, under our reform virtually all workers should be able to receive more in benefits than they expect to receive under the current system. Moreover, at no point in our reform are social security taxes increased. Quite to the contrary, these taxes would be constantly reduced until they are eliminated.

It is true that our results are partly achieved through interim general-revenue financing of social security benefits. But even this need not involve general-revenue tax increases if our reform is enacted as an alternative to other new programs or increased government expenditures.

The primary reason this could be achieved is the wealth creation involved in the private alternative system. The additional wealth created by the investments in this system not only allows benefits equal to those promised by social security to be paid without increased premium payments, but allows even greater benefits to be paid. Both permanent tax increases and benefit cuts could therefore be avoided while solving the program's financing problems and even allowing today's young workers to receive much higher benefits.

We should note that virtually none of the major problems of social security that we have discussed would be solved, or even substantially mitigated, merely by raising payroll taxes or cutting benefits. The inadequate benefits for today's young workers, the negative effects on the economy, the inherent discrimination, the waste of welfare benefits and other negative effects on the poor, the political instability, the coercive structure—all these problems in the current system would continue. The bankruptcy problem might be mitigated, but even this would not be fundamentally solved because the pay-as-you-go nature of the program would remain. In addition, the substantial side benefits of our reform we have noted, such as a broader distribution of national wealth, would not result simply from raising taxes or cutting benefits.

Given all these powerful beneficial effects, our reform proposal would seem well worthwhile. Its only costs are transitory—the need to pay off the resulting deficits in the phase-in period of the reform. But the sacrifices necessary to meet these deficits are minor, especially compared with the benefits. The problems and negative impacts of the current program have become too severe to continue to be tolerated. Social security today is just no longer working. The outdated program must be fundamentally reformed to suit the need of modern Americans.

Politics and Prospects

With these benefits, it is difficult to imagine why anyone would oppose this reform. Basically, since virtually everyone would benefit from the reform, virtually everyone should support it.

Our reform would give both the liberals and the conservatives what they really want. For the liberals, there would be a general revenue-financed welfare program structured to suit the needs of the elderly poor. There is no reason why liberals should otherwise favor forcing individuals to serve their insurance and retirement needs through the current, government-run, social security program, particularly given the enormous drawbacks we have discussed to serving this function through the current program. In addition, for liberals, the reform abolishes the regressive payroll tax, particularly as a means of financing welfare benefits, and general revenues are used to solve the current, short-term financing problems of the program. The reform makes more funds available to the poor by eliminating the current wasteful payment of welfare benefits to those who are not poor. The reform ends the current system's discrimination against minority groups and helps them in the many additional ways described above. The reform results in a more equal distribution of wealth, which should appeal greatly to liberals. Finally, if liberals mean what they say, it will be important to them that the reform increases individual liberty.

Yet conservatives should favor the reform because it denationalizes or privatizes the insurance elements of the current social security program, relying on private market forces to perform this function. Also, for conservatives, the reform reduces taxes and government spending. It improves economic efficiency, increases the role of individual responsibility, and bases benefit payments on what has been earned and paid for, rather than on welfare criteria. Finally, if conservatives mean what they say, it will be important to them that the reform increases individual liberty.

Labor unions should support the reform as well. It would provide workers, particularly young workers, with the opportunity to receive higher benefits for lower payments and to accumulate large amounts of wealth through the higher yielding private alternatives. It would eliminate the bankruptcy problem, which threatens the future financial security of these workers. It would greatly improve the economy in which these workers must earn their living. It would even result in higher wages and more jobs and employment, the chief goals of labor unions. It would also remove a burdensome tax on labor union members and in the long run, if the savings requirement is reduced or phased out, allow them more currently disposable income. It would provide the common man with a large ownership stake in America's business and industry.

In the past, labor unions may have perceived social security as the most feasible way of getting a basic pension plan for their workers. But given the fact that a superior alternative now exists for the provision of these pension benefits, it makes no sense for labor unions to support forcing workers to forgo this superior alternative and remain in the present program. If labor unions fail to support the reform and continue unquestioning support for the current social security program, they will not be pursuing the best interests of their members.

Businesses should also support the reform because it provides more capital investment, improves the economic climate, and increases economic growth. It allows businesses to hire more workers and expand in a growing economy and offers many businesses a new opportunity to provide insurance, savings, and investment plans to new customers.

Minority groups should also favor the reform. It would end discrimination against them and expand their opportunities. Since the poor would also greatly benefit, they and those concerned with their plight should also support the reform.

Young people stand to benefit the most, particularly on a monetary basis. Social security is today becoming a young people's issue, rather than an elderly issue, because the current program is hurting the young the most. The difference between what these workers could receive through the private system and through social security has now become so great, as we have seen, that serious and fundamental reform has become absolutely necessary on these grounds alone. But beyond this, it is today's young workers who are threatened by the long-term financing problems of social security. It is these young workers who must work the rest of their lives in an economy stifled by the program. And it is these young workers who face an endlessly growing, intolerable burden of payroll taxes for the rest of their working years. Young people should therefore be in the forefront in organizing support for the reform.

Finally, the elderly should support the reform as well. The reform, as we have seen, does not involve cutting total benefits in any way. It would instead greatly benefit the elderly by solving the short-term financing problems of the current program and assuring their currently expected benefits. Moreover, the elderly should also be pleased by the benefits of the reform for their children and grandchildren.

Recent public opinion polls suggest the potentially strong public support for our proposed reform. A *Washington Post*-ABC poll taken in 1981[35] found that while the vast majority of Americans opposed raising payroll taxes or cutting benefits, two out of three would support cutting other government programs and using these funds to solve social security's problems, as our proposed reform would do.

The political prospects for the reform are enhanced by the fact that the pay-as-you-go program is now entering the mature phase of its development. The political perception of the program is therefore likely to be quite different in the near future than it has been recently. Now the focus shifts from passing out free benefits through constant, unearned benefit increases, to consistently raising taxes to meet ever-accelerating benefit obligations. The heavy tax burden recently imposed is already turning taxpayers against the program. Many consider current tax levels already intolerable. As voters begin to realize the magnitude of tax increases already scheduled for the future, and as they become aware of the enormous taxes necessary to pay the benefits promised to today's young workers, the traditional popularity of the program may be preserved only in history books.

Furthermore, as the program enters the mature stage, its possible bankruptcy becomes a serious issue, as we have seen. Periodic crises threatening the destruction of the program will cause public confidence in the security of the system to decline and will undermine continued support for the program. A 1982 *Washington Post*-ABC news poll found that already 66 percent of those under 45, and 74 percent of those under 30, believe that the program will not even be in existence when they retire.[36] The same poll found that 75 percent of those between 25 and 34 thought they would not receive the full benefits promised them by the program. A 1981 *New York Times*-CBS poll found that 73 percent of

[35]Barry Sussman, "By 3 to 2 Americans Disapprove of Reagan Plan for Social Security," *Washington Post*, May 16, 1981, p. A8.

[36]Dan Balz, "Public Increasingly Doubts Survival of Social Security," *Washington Post*, February 13, 1982, p. A7.

all Americans had little or no confidence in the system's ability to provide retirement benefits for them or their spouses.[37] This lack of confidence will lead to further political pressures for reform.

Also, as the program matures, the apparent returns an individual receives on his tax dollars paid into the program decline dramatically. The free benefits passed out in the start-up phase make social security appear to be able to pay higher returns than private alternatives. But when these free benefits cease in the mature stage, the benefits paid under social security will, as we have seen, be far less than the benefits available from the private sector. As the loss of these available benefits becomes apparent to voters, the popularity of the program is likely to dissipate further, resulting in additional pressure for reform.

Moreover, as the returns in the social security program fall, the inequities of the system are likely to become more troubling. When everyone is receiving far more than he has paid in taxes, no one is likely to object if some seem to receive more than others for no good reason. But when recipients are already receiving lower returns than they could get elsewhere, they are likely to become quite disturbed if some are receiving an inequitable share of the already inadequate benefits. The inequities of the program therefore will become more troubling, and support for the program will be further undermined.

These factors indicate that in the near future social security will be a whole new ball game politically. For those politicians unprepared to offer new approaches, the program will present nothing but potential trouble. This situation is already rapidly developing. The political realities are that the public is now, and will be even more so in the near future, ready for a serious reappraisal of our social security system and, if a good plan is offered, ready for broad, fundamental reform.

Conclusion

We have presented in this chapter a proposal for reform that will separate the welfare from the insurance elements of the current social security system and privatize the insurance elements. This proposal does, as promised, offer a reform that:

1) solves all the major problems of the program;
2) gives the liberals and the conservatives what they really want;
3) should receive the broad support of the American public; and
4) accomplishes all this without cutting social security benefits or raising social security taxes.

[37]Ibid.

But whether this reform proposal is adopted or not, basic and fundamental reform of social security is inevitable because the program cannot continue as it is currently structured. As we have seen, the Social Security Administration's own projections of the future financial status of the program indicate that further large tax increases will be necessary to meet the program's benefit obligations. To pay the benefits currently being promised to young workers entering the work force today, tax rates will have to be raised to between 25 percent and 33 percent of taxable payroll, as compared with 13 percent today. The government's own projections also indicate that even in the shortterm, the program is likely to be unable to meet all its benefit obligations by 1983 or 1984.

In response to this developing short-term financing crisis, the public will probably not be willing to accept the stiff tax increases necessary to bail out the program. Voters have just swallowed the largest tax increase in history, passed in 1977, which was intended to solve the short-term financing crises of the late 1970s. Indeed, the 1977 tax increases have not been fully phased in, nor is the public generally aware that future tax increases are already on the books, yet the public has already complained loudly about those tax increases that have taken effect. Already there has been considerable talk of a tax rollback. Legislators have even begun to advance such bizarre schemes as using a windfall profits tax on oil to finance social security. The necessity for even further, overwhelming, tax increases to solve the long-term financing problem will further discourage voters from accepting short-term tax increases to save the system.

Cutting benefits, however, is likely to be as politically unpopular as raising taxes. In response to these problems, therefore, Congress is most likely to end up subsidizing the program from general revenues, unless it adopts our proposed reform. Once this occurs, political pressure will develop to increase reliance on the progressive income tax and decrease reliance on the regressive payroll tax. Thus, a larger and larger portion of the program will be financed from general revenues.

Such general-revenue financing will result in further political pressure to require a means test for social security benefits. People will ask why benefits should be paid out of general revenues to those who are not poor or in need. The concept of earned entitlement to social security benefits will have been destroyed. Political pressure to tighten this means test will continue until only the poor or the near poor are eligible for social security benefits.

At this point, the welfare function will have been separated from the insurance function, with the latter privatized. This end result will inevitably occur merely from continuing social security on its present course. The current program's days are numbered. The program as it is now structured is unstable. It will be basically and fundamentally reformed. The only question is whether it will be done in this haphazard, unplanned, unintentional way, which will waste valuable time and unnecessarily drag out several of the program's negative impacts, or whether it will be done through a planned, orderly, phased-in approach in advance.

The simple truth is that given the current structure of the program, "the social security problem will return like Banquo's ghost until really serious and courageous efforts are made to solve it."[38]

---

[38]"Back So Soon?," *Wall Street Journal*, April 1979, p. 26.

APPENDIX

TABLE 1

Social Security Tax Rates[1]
(percentage of taxable payroll)

	Employee & Employer Combined					Self-Employed				
	OASI	DI	HI	OASDI	OASDHI	OASI	DI	HI	OASDI	OASDHI
1937	2.00	—	—	—	—	—	—	—	—	—
1938	2.00	—	—	—	—	—	—	—	—	—
1939	2.00	—	—	—	—	—	—	—	—	—
1940	2.00	—	—	—	—	—	—	—	—	—
1941	2.00	—	—	—	—	—	—	—	—	—
1942	2.00	—	—	—	—	—	—	—	—	—
1943	2.00	—	—	—	—	—	—	—	—	—
1944	2.00	—	—	—	—	—	—	—	—	—
1945	2.00	—	—	—	—	—	—	—	—	—
1946	2.00	—	—	—	—	—	—	—	—	—
1947	2.00	—	—	—	—	—	—	—	—	—
1948	2.00	—	—	—	—	—	—	—	—	—
1949	2.00	—	—	—	—	—	—	—	—	—
1950	3.00	—	—	—	—	—	—	—	—	—
1951	3.00	—	—	—	—	2.25	—	—	—	—
1952	3.00	—	—	—	—	2.25	—	—	—	—
1953	3.00	—	—	—	—	2.25	—	—	—	—
1954	4.00	—	—	—	—	3.00	—	—	—	—
1955	4.00	—	—	—	—	3.00	—	—	—	—
1956	4.00	—	—	—	—	3.00	—	—	—	—
1957	4.00	0.50	—	4.50	—	3.00	0.375	—	3.375	—
1958	4.00	0.50	—	4.50	—	3.00	0.375	—	3.375	—
1959	4.50	0.50	—	5.00	—	3.375	0.375	—	3.75	—
1960	5.50	0.50	—	6.00	—	4.125	0.375	—	4.50	—
1961	5.50	0.50	—	6.00	—	4.125	0.375	—	4.50	—
1962	5.75	0.50	—	6.25	—	4.325	0.375	—	4.70	—
1963	6.75	0.50	—	7.25	—	5.025	0.375	—	5.40	—
1964	6.75	0.50	—	7.25	—	5.025	0.375	—	5.40	—
1965	6.75	0.50	—	7.25	—	5.025	0.375	—	5.40	—
1966	7.00	0.70	0.70	7.70	8.40	5.275	0.525	0.35	5.80	6.15
1967	7.10	0.70	1.00	7.80	8.00	5.375	0.525	0.50	5.90	6.40
1968	6.65	0.95	1.20	7.60	8.80	5.0875	0.7125	0.60	5.80	6.40
1969	7.45	0.95	1.20	8.40	9.60	5.5875	0.7125	0.60	6.30	6.90
1970	7.30	1.10	1.20	8.40	9.60	5.475	0.825	0.60	6.30	6.90
1971	8.10	1.10	1.20	9.20	10.40	6.075	0.825	0.60	6.90	7.50
1972	8.10	1.10	1.20	9.20	10.40	6.075	0.825	0.60	6.90	7.50
1973	8.60	1.10	2.00	9.70	11.70	6.205	0.795	1.00	7.00	8.00
1974	8.75	1.15	1.80	9.90	11.70	6.185	0.815	0.90	7.00	7.90
1975	8.75	1.15	1.80	9.90	11.70	6.185	0.815	0.90	7.00	7.90
1976	8.75	1.15	1.80	9.90	11.70	6.185	0.815	0.90	7.00	7.90
1977	8.75	1.15	1.80	9.90	11.70	6.185	0.815	0.90	7.00	7.90
1978	8.55	1.55	2.00	10.10	12.10	6.01	1.09	1.00	7.10	8.10
1979	8.66	1.50	2.10	10.16	12.26	6.01	1.04	1.05	7.05	8.10

(cont. on next page)

TABLE 1 (continued)

	Employee & Employer Combined					Self-Employed				
	OASI	DI	HI	OASDI	OASDHI	OASI	DI	HI	OASDI	OASDHI
1980	8.66	1.50	2.10	10.16	12.26	6.01	1.04	1.05	7.05	8.10
1981	9.05	1.65	2.60	10.70	13.30	6.7625	1.2375	1.30	8.00	9.30
1982	9.15	1.65	2.60	10.80	13.40	6.8125	1.2375	1.30	8.05	9.35
1983	9.15	1.65	2.60	10.80	13.40	6.8125	1.2375	1.30	8.05	9.35
1984	9.15	1.65	2.60	10.80	13.40	6.8125	1.2375	1.30	8.05	9.35
1985	9.50	1.90	2.70	11.40	14.10	7.125	1.425	1.35	8.55	9.9
1986	9.50	1.90	2.90	11.40	14.30	7.125	1.425	1.45	8.55	10.00
1987	9.50	1.90	2.90	11.40	14.30	7.125	1.425	1.45	8.55	10.00
1988	9.50	1.90	2.90	11.40	14.30	7.125	1.425	1.45	8.55	10.00
1989	9.50	1.90	2.90	11.40	14.30	7.125	1.425	1.45	8.55	10.00
1990 and later	10.20	2.20	2.90	12.40	15.30	7.650	1.650	1.45	9.30	10.75

SOURCE: Social Security Board of Trustees, *1982 Annual Report of the Federal Old-Age and Survivors Insurance and Disability Insurance Trust Funds* (Washington, D.C., April 1, 1982); Social Security Board of Trustees, *1982 Annual Report of the Federal Hospital Insurance Trust Fund* (Washington, D.C., April 1, 1982).

[1]Figures for 1983 and beyond are as provided in current law.

TABLE 2

Maximum Social Security Tax[1]
(employer and employee shares)

	Maximum Taxable Income	Maximum Tax OASI	Maximum Tax OASDI	Maximum Tax OASDHI		Maximum Taxable Income	Maximum Tax OASI	Maximum Tax OASDI	Maximum Tax OASDHI
1937	3,000	60	—	—	1965	4,800	324	348	—
1938	3,000	60	—	—	1966	6,600	462	508.20	554.20
1939	3,000	60	—	—	1967	6,600	468.60	514.80	580.80
1940	3,000	60	—	—	1968	7,800	518.70	592.80	686.40
1941	3,000	60	—	—	1969	7,800	581.10	655.20	748.80
1942	3,000	60	—	—	1970	7,800	569.40	655.20	748.80
1943	3,000	60	—	—	1971	7,800	631.80	717.60	811.20
1944	3,000	60	—	—	1972	9,000	729.00	828.00	936.00
1945	3,000	60	—	—	1973	10,800	928.80	1047.60	1263.60
1946	3,000	60	—	—	1974	13,200	1155.00	1306.80	1544.40
1947	3,000	60	—	—	1975	14,100	1233.75	1395.90	1649.70
1948	3,000	60	—	—	1976	15,300	1338.75	1514.70	1790.10
1949	3,000	60	—	—	1977	16,500	1443.78	1633.50	1930.50
1950	3,000	90	—	—	1978	17,700	1513.35	1787.70	2141.70
1951	3,600	108	—	—	1979	22,900	1983.14	2326.64	2807.54
1952	3,600	108	—	—	1980	25,900	2242.94	2631.44	3175.34
1953	3,600	108	—	—	1981	29,700	2687.85	3177.90	3950.10
1954	3,600	144	—	—	1982	32,400	2964.60	3499.20	4341.60
1955	4,200	168	—	—	1983[2]	35,100	3211.65	3790.80	4703.40
1956	4,200	168	—	—	1984	37,500	3431.25	4050.00	5025.00
1957	4,200	168	189	—	1985	40,500	3847.50	4617.00	5710.50
1958	4,200	168	189	—	1986	43,800	4161.00	4993.20	6263.40

(cont. on next page)

TABLE 2 (continued)

	Maximum Taxable Income	Maximum Tax		
		OASI	OASDI	OASDHI
1959	4,800	216	240	—
1960	4,800	264	288	—
1961	4,800	264	288	—
1962	4,800	276	300	—
1963	4,800	324	348	—
1964	4,800	324	348	—

	Maximum Taxable Income	Maximum Tax		
		OASI	OASDI	OASDHI
1987	46,800	4446.00	5335.20	6692.40
1988	50,000	4750.00	5700.00	7150.00
1989	53,300	5063.50	6076.20	7621.90
1990	56,800	5793.60	7043.20	8690.40

SOURCE: Social Security Administration, *Social Security Bulletin: Annual Statistical Supplement, 1980* (Washington, D.C.: U.S. Government Printing Office, 1982); Social Security Board of Trustees, *1982 Annual Report of the Board of Trustees of the Federal Old-Age and Survivors Insurance and Disability Insurance Trust Funds* (Washington, D.C., April 1, 1982); Social Security Board of Trustees, *1982 Annual Report of the Board of Trustees of the Federal Hospital Insurance Trust Funds* (Washington, D.C., April 1, 1982).

[1]Figures in dollars.

[2]Projections 1983–1990 based on Social Security Board of Trustees Assumptions, Alternative II 1982 Annual Reports.

TABLE 3

Social Security Taxes and Other Federal Taxes[1]

	Total Federal Government Receipts	Personal Tax Receipts	Corporate Profits Tax and Indirect Business Tax and Non-Tax Accruals	Other Social Insurance Taxes	Social Security Taxes			as a percent of total federal taxes
					OASI	OASDI	OASDHI	
1937	7.0	1.7	3.7	0.8	0.8	—	—	11.4%
1938	6.5	1.6	3.1	1.3	0.4	—	—	6.2%
1939	6.7	1.2	3.6	1.3	0.6	—	—	9.0%
1940	8.6	1.4	5.3	1.7	0.3	—	—	3.5%
1941	15.4	2.0	10.9	1.7	0.8	—	—	5.2%
1942	22.9	4.7	15.1	2.2	1.0	—	—	4.4%
1943	39.3	16.5	18.6	3.0	1.2	—	—	3.1%
1944	41.0	17.5	18.7	3.5	1.3	—	—	3.2%
1945	42.5	19.4	17.4	4.5	1.3	—	—	3.1%
1946	39.1	17.2	16.4	4.2	1.3	—	—	3.3%
1947	43.2	19.6	18.5	3.5	1.6	—	—	3.7%
1948	43.2	19.0	19.7	2.8	1.7	—	—	3.9%
1949	38.7	16.1	17.6	3.2	1.7	—	—	4.4%
1950	50.0	18.1	26.0	3.2	2.7	—	—	5.4%
1951	64.3	26.1	31.0	3.7	3.4	—	—	5.3%
1952	67.3	31.0	28.9	3.6	3.8	—	—.	5.6%
1953	70.0	32.2	30.4	3.5	3.9	—	—	5.6%
1954	63.7	29.0	26.6	3.0	5.2	—	—	8.2%
1955	72.6	31.4	31.8	3.7	5.7	—	—	7.9%
1956	78.0	35.2	32.1	4.4	6.2	—	—	7.9%
1957	81.9	37.4	32.2	4.8	6.8	7.5	—	9.2%
1958	78.7	36.8	29.5	3.9	7.6	8.5	—	10.8%
1959	89.8	39.9	35.0	6.0	8.1	8.9	—	9.9%
1960	96.1	43.6	34.8	5.7	10.9	11.9	—	12.4%
1961	98.1	44.7	35.1	6.0	11.3	12.3	—	12.5%
1962	106.2	48.6	37.1	7.4	12.1	13.1	—	12.3%
1963	114.4	51.5	39.9	7.5	14.5	15.6	—	13.6%
1964	114.9	48.6	42.3	7.2	15.7	16.8	—	14.6%
1965	124.3	53.9	45.4	7.8	16.0	17.2	—	13.8%
1966	141.8	61.7	47.0	8.6	20.6	22.6	24.5	17.3%
1967	150.5	67.5	46.3	8.1	23.1	25.4	28.6	19.0%
1968	174.4	79.7	54.1	9.5	23.7	27.0	31.2	17.9%
1969	196.9	95.1	55.1	10.7	27.9	31.5	36.0	18.3%
1970	191.9	92.6	49.9	9.6	30.3	34.7	39.7	20.7%
1971	198.6	90.3	53.9	11.1	33.7	38.3	43.3	21.8%
1972	227.5	108.2	56.6	14.0	37.8	42.9	48.7	21.4%
1973	258.6	114.7	64.5	17.6	46.0	51.9	61.9	23.9%
1974	287.8	131.3	66.8	19.9	52.1	58.9	69.9	24.3%
1975	287.3	125.8	67.5	18.2	56.8	64.3	75.9	26.4%
1976	331.8	147.3	78.0	22.2	63.4	71.6	84.3	25.4%
1977	375.1	170.1	86.6	25.7	69.6	78.7	92.8	24.7%
1978	431.5	194.9	99.3	31.0	75.5	88.9	106.2	24.6%
1979	494.4	231.4	104.0	35.2	87.9	103.0	123.8	25.0%
1980	540.8	257.8	110.8	31.6	103.5	116.7	140.6	26.0%
1981	624.8	296.2	126.2	30.2	122.6	139.4	172.3	27.6%
1982[2]	—	—	—	—	137.1	146.3	181.0	—

(cont. on next page)

TABLE 3 (continued)

SOURCE: National Income and Product Accounts, 1929–1974; President's Council of Economic Advisers, *1982 Economic Report of the President* (Washington, D.C.: U.S. Government Printing Office, 1982); Social Security Board of Trustees, *1982 Annual Report of the Board of Trustees of the Federal Hospital Insurance Trust Funds* (Washington, D.C., April 1, 1982).

[1]All figures are in billions, except those in the last column which are presented as percentages.

[2]Figures are projections made by the Social Security Board of Trustees, 1982 Annual Reports, Alternative IIB assumptions.

TABLE 4

Social Security Expenditures and Other Federal Expenditures[1]

	Total Federal Government Expenditure	Non-Social Security Transfer Payments	Federal Purchases of Goods and Services	Total Social Security Expenditures			
				OASI	OASDI	OASDHI	as a percent of total fed. expenditures
1937	7.4	0.9	4.7	0.001	—	—	0.01%
1938	8.6	1.2	5.5	0.01	—	—	0.1%
1939	8.9	1.3	5.2	0.01	—	—	0.1%
1940	10.0	1.4	6.1	0.06	—	—	0.6%
1941	20.5	1.3	16.9	0.1	—	—	0.5%
1942	56.1	1.4	52.0	0.2	—	—	0.4%
1943	85.8	1.0	81.3	0.2	—	—	0.2%
1944	95.5	1.5	89.4	0.2	—	—	0.2%
1945	84.6	4.4	74.6	0.3	—	—	0.4%
1946	35.6	11.0	17.6	0.4	—	—	1.1%
1947	29.8	10.3	12.7	0.5	—	—	1.7%
1948	34.9	10.9	16.7	0.6	—	—	1.7%
1949	41.3	13.1	20.4	0.7	—	—	1.7%
1950	40.8	13.4	18.7	1.0	—	—	2.5%
1951	57.8	9.7	38.3	2.0	—	—	3.5%
1952	71.1	8.6	52.4	2.3	—	—	3.2%
1953	77.1	8.3	57.5	3.1	—	—	4.0%
1954	69.8	9.6	47.9	3.7	—	—	5.3%
1955	68.1	9.3	44.5	5.1	—	—	7.5%
1956	71.9	9.5	45.9	5.8	—	—	8.1%
1957	79.6	9.9	50.0	7.5	7.6	—	9.5%
1958	88.9	12.5	53.9	8.6	8.9	—	10.0%
1959	91.0	11.1	53.9	10.3	10.8	—	11.9%
1960	93.1	11.7	53.7	11.2	11.8	—	12.7%
1961	101.9	13.7	57.4	12.4	13.4	—	13.2%
1962	110.4	12.6	63.7	14.0	15.2	—	13.8%
1963	114.2	13.0	64.6	14.9	16.2	—	14.2%
1964	118.2	13.1	65.2	15.6	17.0	—	14.4%
1965	123.8	13.3	67.3	17.5	19.2	—	15.5%
1966	143.6	13.9	78.8	19.0	20.9	21.9	15.3%
1967	163.7	16.4	90.9	20.4	22.5	25.9	15.8%
1968	180.5	17.8	98.0	23.6	26.0	30.3	16.8%
1969	188.4	20.0	97.6	25.2	27.9	32.7	17.4%
1970	204.3	25.1	95.7	29.8	33.1	38.4	18.8%
1971	220.6	30.9	96.2	34.5	38.5	44.4	20.1%
1972	244.3	39.9	101.7	38.5	43.3	49.8	20.4%
1973	264.2	35.5	102.0	47.2	53.1	60.4	22.9%
1974	299.3	47.7	111.0	53.4	60.6	70.0	23.4%
1975	356.6	68.6	122.7	60.4	69.2	80.8	22.7%
1976	384.8	70.1	129.2	67.9	78.2	91.9	23.9%
1977	421.5	69.5	143.9	75.3	87.3	103.3	24.5%
1978	460.7	71.2	153.4	83.1	96.0	114.4	24.8%

(cont. on next page)

TABLE 4 (continued)

	Total Federal Government Expenditure	Non-Social Security Transfer Payments	Federal Purchases of Goods and Services	Total Social Security Expenditures			
				OASI	OASDI	OASDHI	as a percent of total fed. expenditures
1979	509.2	80.7	167.9	93.1	107.3	128.4	25.2%
1980	602.0	100.6	198.9	107.7	123.6	149.1	24.8%
1981	686.4	109.3	228.6	126.7	144.4	175.1	25.5%
1982[2]	—	—	—	141.8	160.3	195.9	—

SOURCE: National Income and Product Accounts, 1929–1974; President's Council of Economic Advisers, *1982 Annual Report of the President* (Washington, D.C.: U.S. Government Printing Office, 1982); Social Security Board of Trustees, *1982 Annual Report of the Board of Trustees of the Federal Old-Age and Survivors Insurance and Disability Insurance Trust Fund* (Washington, D.C., April 1, 1982); Social Security Board of Trustees, *1982 Annual Report of the Board of Trustees of the Federal Hospital Insurance Trust Fund* (Washington, D.C., April 1, 1982).

[1]All figures in billions, except those in the last column, which are presented as percentages.

[2]Figures are projections made by the Social Security Board of Trustees, 1982 Annual Reports, Alternative IIB assumptions.

TABLE 5
The Social Security Trust Funds[1]

	OASI Trust Fund Total Assets	OASI Total Expenditures	OASI Trust Fund as a Percent of Annual OASI Expenditures	OASDI Trust Fund Total Assets	OASDI Total Expenditures	OASDI Trust Fund as a Percent of Annual OASDI Expenditures	OASDHI Trust Fund Total Assets	OASDHI Total Expenditures	OASDHI Trust Fund as a Percent of Annual OASDHI Expenditures
1937	0.8	0.001	80,000%	—	—	—	—	—	—
1938	1.1	0.01	11,000%	—	—	—	—	—	—
1939	1.7	0.01	17,000%	—	—	—	—	—	—
1940	2.0	0.06	3,333%	—	—	—	—	—	—
1941	2.8	0.1	2,800%	—	—	—	—	—	—
1942	3.7	0.2	1,850%	—	—	—	—	—	—
1943	4.8	0.2	2,400%	—	—	—	—	—	—
1944	6.0	0.2	3,000%	—	—	—	—	—	—
1945	7.1	0.3	2,367%	—	—	—	—	—	—
1946	8.2	0.4	2,050%	—	—	—	—	—	—
1947	9.4	0.5	1,880%	—	—	—	—	—	—
1948	10.7	0.6	1,783%	—	—	—	—	—	—
1949	11.8	0.7	1,686%	—	—	—	—	—	—
1950	13.7	1.0	1,370%	—	—	—	—	—	—
1951	15.5	2.0	775%	—	—	—	—	—	—
1952	17.4	2.3	757%	—	—	—	—	—	—
1953	18.7	3.1	603%	—	—	—	—	—	—
1954	20.6	3.7	557%	—	—	—	—	—	—
1955	21.7	5.1	425%	—	—	—	—	—	—
1956	22.5	5.8	388%	—	—	—	—	—	—
1957	22.4	7.5	299%	23.0	7.6	303%	—	—	—

(cont. on next page)

145

TABLE 5 (continued)

Year	OASI Trust Fund Total Assets	OASI Total Expenditures	OASI Trust Fund as a Percent of Annual OASI Expenditures	OASDI Trust Fund Total Assets	OASDI Total Expenditures	OASDI Trust Fund as a Percent of Annual OASDI Expenditures	OASDHI Trust Fund Total Assets	OASDHI Total Expenditures	OASDHI Trust Fund as a Percent of Annual OASDHI Expenditures
1958	21.9	8.6	255%	23.2	8.9	261%	—	—	—
1959	20.1	10.3	195%	22.0	10.8	204%	—	—	—
1960	20.3	11.2	181%	22.6	11.8	192%	—	—	—
1961	19.7	12.4	159%	22.2	13.4	166%	—	—	—
1962	18.3	14.0	131%	20.7	15.2	136%	—	—	—
1963	18.5	14.9	124%	20.7	16.2	128%	—	—	—
1964	19.1	15.6	122%	21.2	17.0	125%	—	—	—
1965	18.2	17.5	104%	19.8	19.2	103%	—	—	—
1966	20.6	19.0	108%	22.3	20.9	107%	23.3	21.9	106%
1967	24.2	20.4	119%	26.3	22.5	117%	27.3	25.9	105%
1968	25.7	23.6	109%	28.7	26.0	110%	30.8	30.3	102%
1969	30.1	25.2	119%	34.2	27.9	123%	36.7	32.7	112%
1970	32.5	29.8	109%	38.1	33.1	115%	41.3	38.4	108%
1971	33.8	34.5	98%	40.4	38.5	105%	43.5	44.4	98%
1972	35.3	38.5	92%	42.8	43.3	99%	45.7	49.8	92%
1973	36.5	47.2	77%	44.4	53.1	84%	50.9	60.4	84%
1974	37.8	53.4	71%	45.9	60.6	76%	55.0	70.0	79%
1975	37.0	60.4	61%	44.3	69.2	64%	54.9	80.8	68%
1976	35.4	67.9	52%	41.1	78.2	53%	51.7	91.9	56%
1977	32.5	75.3	43%	35.9	87.3	41%	46.3	103.3	45%
1978	27.5	83.1	33%	31.7	96.0	33%	43.2	114.2	38%
1979	24.7	93.1	27%	30.3	107.3	28%	43.5	128.4	34%
1980	22.8	107.7	21%	26.5	123.6	21%	40.2	149.1	27%
1981	21.5	126.7	17%	24.5	144.4	17%	43.3	175.1	25%

¹Figures in billions.

TABLE 6

Unfunded Liability and the Trust Funds[1]

	Unfunded Liability for the OASDI Program	OASDI Trust Funds	Trust Funds as a Percent of the Unfunded Liability
1981	5,858	24.5	0.42%
1980	5,601	26.5	0.46%
1979	4,225	30.3	0.72%
1978	3,971	31.7	0.80%
1977	5,362	35.9	0.67%
1976	4,148	41.1	0.99%
1975	2,710	44.3	1.63%
1974	2,460	45.9	1.87%
1973	2,118	44.4	2.10%
1972	1,865	42.8	2.29%
1971	435	40.4	9.29%
1970	415	38.1	9.18%
1969	330	34.2	10.36%
1968	414	28.7	6.93%
1967	350	26.3	7.51%

SOURCE: U.S. Treasury Department, *Statement of Liabilities and Other Financial Commitments of the United States Government* (Saltonstall Report), 1967–1981.

[1]Figures in billions.

TABLE 7

Total Benefit Payments[1]

	OASI	OAA-SSI		OASI	OAA-SSI
1937	1	224	1959	9,842	1,621
1938	10	360	1960	10,677	1,626
1939	14	418	1961	11,862	1,569
1940	35	450	1962	13,356	1,566
1941	88	505	1963	14,217	1,610
1942	131	569	1964	14,914	1,607
1943	166	617	1965	16,737	1,594
1944	209	679	1966	18,267	1,630
1945	274	702	1967	19,468	1,698
1946	378	762	1968	22,642	1,673
1947	466	910	1969	24,209	1,747
1948	556	1,038	1970	28,796	1,866
1949	667	1,259	1971	33,143	1,920
1950	961	1,454	1972	37,122	1,894
1951	1,885	1,428	1973	45,741	1,749
1952	2,194	1,463	1974	51,618	2,414
1953	3,006	1,513	1975	58,509	2,517
1954	3,670	1,498	1976	65,699	2,420
1955	4,968	1,488	1977	73,133	2,364
1956	5,715	1,529	1978	80,352	2,342
1957	7,347	1,609	1979	90,556	2,421
1958	8,327	1,647			

SOURCE: Social Security Administration, *Social Security Bulletin: Annual Statistical Supplement, 1982* (Washington, D.C.: U.S. Government Printing Office, 1982); Social Security Board of Trustees, *1982 Annual Report of the Board of Trustees of the Federal Old-Age and Survivors Insurance and Disability Insurance Trust Funds* (Washington, D.C., April 1, 1982); Social Security Board of Trustees, *1982 Annual Report of the Board of Trustees of the Federal Hospital Insurance Trust Funds* (Washington, D.C., April 1, 1982), U.S. Department of Health, Education and Welfare.

[1]Figures in millions.

TABLE 8

Maximum Income, Alternative III
Benefits Which Can Be Paid by Private System[1]

Real Rates of Return	Retirement Trust Fund Accumulated at Age 65	Perpetual Annuity	Life Annuity Single Worker	Life Annuity, Couple	
				both spouses alive	one spouse alive
3.0%	478,746	14,362 (31%)	43,648 (95%)	36,377 (79%)	24,251 (53%)
3.5%	541,403	18,949 (41%)	51,307 (111%)	43,015 (93%)	28,677 (62%)
4.0%	612,459	24,498 (53%)	60,264 (130%)	50,811 (110%)	33,874 (73%)
4.5%	693,437	31,205 (68%)	70,769 (153%)	59,993 (130%)	39,996 (87%)
5.0%	786,233	39,312 (85%)	83,138 (180%)	70,846 (153%)	47,231 (102%)
5.5%	892,792	49,104 (106%)	97,720 (211%)	83,686 (181%)	55,791 (121%)
6.0%	1,015,403	60,924 (132%)	114,932 (248%)	98,895 (214%)	65,930 (143%)
6.5%	1,156,709	75,186 (162%)	135,270 (292%)	116,925 (253%)	77,950 (168%)
7.0%	1,319,891	92,392 (200%)	159,333 (344%)	138,325 (299%)	92,217 (199%)
7.5%	1,508,361	113,127 (244%)	187,800 (405%)	163,718 (353%)	109,145 (236%)
8.0%	1,726,449	138,116 (298%)	221,521 (478%)	193,884 (418%)	129,256 (279%)

Social Security Pays: Single Worker—12,525 (27%)
Couple, Both Spouses Alive—18,787 (41%)
Couple, One Spouse Alive—12,525 (27%)

[1]All figures in constant 1980 dollars, replacement ratios in parentheses.

TABLE 9

Average Income, Alternative III
Benefits Which Can Be Paid by Private System[1]

Real Rates of Return	Retirement Trust Fund Accumulated at Age 65	Perpetual Annuity	Life Annuity Single Worker	Life Annuity, Couple	
				both spouses alive	one spouse alive
3.0%	209,519	6,286 (31%)	19,102 (94%)	15,920 (78%)	10,613 (52%)
3.5%	243,337	8,517 (42%)	23,060 (113%)	19,333 (95%)	12,889 (63%)
4.0%	280,379	11,215 (55%)	27,588 (135%)	23,261 (114%)	15,507 (76%)
4.5%	322,025	14,491 (71%)	32,864 (161%)	27,860 (137%)	18,574 (91%)
5.0%	369,574	18,479 (91%)	39,080 (191%)	33,302 (163%)	22,201 (109%)
5.5%	424,423	23,343 (114%)	46,455 (227%)	39,783 (195%)	26,522 (130%)
6.0%	488,008	29,281 (143%)	55,237 (270%)	47,530 (232%)	31,686 (155%)
6.5%	561,834	36,519 (179%)	65,703 (321%)	56,793 (278%)	37,862 (185%)
7.0%	647,797	45,346 (222%)	78,200 (382%)	67,889 (332%)	45,260 (221%)
7.5%	747,945	56,096 (274%)	93,124 (454%)	81,182 (397%)	54,122 (264%)
8.0%	864,844	69,188 (338%)	110,968 (541%)	97,124 (474%)	64,749 (316%)

Social Security Pays: Single Worker—8,172 (40%)
Couple, Both Spouses Alive—12,258 (60%)
Couple, One Spouse Alive—8,172 (40%)

[1]All figures in constant 1980 dollars, replacement ratios in parentheses.

150

TABLE 10

Low Income, Alternative III
Benefits Which Can Be Paid by Private System[1]

Real Rates of Return	Retirement Trust Fund Accumulated at Age 65	Perpetual Annuity	Life Annuity Single Worker	Life Annuity, Couple	
				both spouses alive	one spouse alive
3.0%	113,592	3,408 (34%)	10,356 (103%)	8,631 (86%)	5,754 (57%)
3.5%	136,050	4,762 (48%)	12,893 (128%)	10,809 (108%)	7,206 (72%)
4.0%	160,270	6,411 (64%)	15,770 (156%)	13,297 (132%)	8,864 (88%)
4.5%	187,407	8,433 (84%)	19,126 (190%)	16,214 (161%)	10,809 (107%)
5.0%	218,608	10,930 (109%)	23,116 (229%)	19,698 (195%)	13,132 (130%)
5.5%	254,961	14,023 (139%)	27,906 (276%)	23,899 (237%)	15,933 (158%)
6.0%	297,609	17,857 (177%)	33,686 (333%)	28,986 (287%)	19,324 (192%)
6.5%	347,900	22,613 (224%)	40,685 (403%)	35,167 (348%)	23,445 (232%)
7.0%	407,362	28,515 (282%)	49,175 (487%)	42,692 (423%)	28,461 (282%)
7.5%	477,806	35,835 (355%)	59,490 (589%)	51,861 (513%)	34,574 (342%)
8.0%	561,387	44,911 (444%)	72,032 (713%)	63,045 (624%)	42,030 (416%)

Social Security Pays: Single Worker—5,270 (53%)
Couple, Both Spouses Alive—7,905 (79%)
Couple, One Spouse Alive—5,270 (53%)

[1]All figures in constant 1980 dollars, replacement ratios in parentheses.

TABLE 11

Maximum Income, Alternative II
Benefits Which Can Be Paid by Private System[1]

Real Rates of Return	Retirement Trust Fund Accumulated at Age 65	Perpetual Annuity	Life Annuity Single Worker	Life Annuity, Couple	
				both spouses alive	one spouse alive
3.0%	471,291	14,139 (25%)	42,968 (75%)	35,810 (63%)	23,874 (42%)
3.5%	534,491	18,707 (33%)	50,652 (88%)	42,466 (74%)	28,311 (49%)
4.0%	604,579	24,183 (42%)	59,489 (103%)	50,158 (87%)	33,439 (58%)
4.5%	683,728	30,768 (54%)	69,778 (121%)	59,153 (103%)	39,436 (69%)
5.0%	773,905	38,695 (67%)	81,834 (142%)	69,735 (121%)	46,490 (81%)
5.5%	877,072	48,239 (84%)	95,999 (166%)	82,213 (143%)	54,808 (95%)
6.0%	995,320	59,719 (104%)	112,659 (195%)	96,939 (168%)	64,626 (112%)
6.5%	1,131,319	73,536 (127%)	132,300 (229%)	114,359 (198%)	76,239 (132%)
7.0%	1,287,924	90,155 (156%)	155,474 (269%)	134,975 (234%)	89,983 (156%)
7.5%	1,468,488	110,137 (191%)	182,836 (316%)	159,390 (276%)	106,260 (184%)
8.0%	1,677,025	134,162 (232%)	215,179 (372%)	188,334 (326%)	125,556 (217%)

Social Security Pays: Single Worker—15,551 (27%)
Couple, Both Spouses Alive—23,326 (41%)
Couple, One Spouse Alive—15,551 (27%)

[1]All figures in constant 1980 dollars, replacement ratios in parentheses.

TABLE 12

Average Income, Alternative II
Benefits Which Can Be Paid by Private System[1]

Real Rates of Return	Retirement Trust Fund Accumulated at Age 65	Perpetual Annuity	Life Annuity Single Worker	Life Annuity, Couple	
				both spouses alive	one spouse alive
3.0%	192,998	5,790 (23%)	17,596 (69%)	14,665 (58%)	9,776 (39%)
3.5%	229,526	8,033 (32%)	21,752 (85%)	18,236 (72%)	12,157 (48%)
4.0%	268,202	10,728 (42%)	26,390 (103%)	22,251 (87%)	14,834 (58%)
4.5%	309,887	13,945 (55%)	31,626 (124%)	26,810 (105%)	17,873 (70%)
5.0%	356,349	17,817 (70%)	37,681 (147%)	32,110 (126%)	21,407 (84%)
5.5%	409,107	22,501 (88%)	44,778 (175%)	38,348 (150%)	25,565 (100%)
6.0%	469,662	28,180 (110%)	53,160 (208%)	45,743 (179%)	30,495 (119%)
6.5%	539,738	35,083 (137%)	63,119 (247%)	54,559 (213%)	36,373 (142%)
7.0%	621,077	43,475 (170%)	74,974 (293%)	65,089 (254%)	43,393 (170%)
7.5%	715,586	53,669 (210%)	89,095 (348%)	77,670 (304%)	51,780 (202%)
8.0%	825,688	66,055 (258%)	105,944 (413%)	92,727 (362%)	61,818 (241%)

Social Security Pays: Single Worker—10,272 (40%)
Couple, Both Spouses Alive—15,408 (60%)
Couple, One Spouse Alive—10,272 (40%)

[1]All figures in constant 1980 dollars, replacement ratios in parentheses.

TABLE 13

Low Income, Alternative II
Benefits Which Can Be Paid by Private System[1]

Real Rates of Return	Retirement Trust Fund Accumulated at Age 65	Perpetual Annuity	Life Annuity Single Worker	Life Annuity, Couple	
				both spouses alive	one spouse alive
3.0%	101,927	3,058 (24%)	9,293 (73%)	7,745 (61%)	5,163 (41%)
3.5%	125,802	4,403 (35%)	11,922 (93%)	9,995 (78%)	6,663 (52%)
4.0%	152,231	6,089 (48%)	14,979 (117%)	12,630 (99%)	8,420 (66%)
4.5%	180,365	8,116 (63%)	18,407 (143%)	15,605 (122%)	10,403 (81%)
5.0%	211,436	10,572 (82%)	22,358 (174%)	19,052 (148%)	12,701 (99%)
5.5%	246,801	13,574 (106%)	27,013 (210%)	23,134 (180%)	15,423 (120%)
6.0%	287,798	17,268 (134%)	32,575 (253%)	28,030 (218%)	18,687 (145%)
6.5%	335,798	21,827 (170%)	39,269 (305%)	33,944 (264%)	22,629 (176%)
7.0%	392,233	27,456 (213%)	47,349 (368%)	41,106 (319%)	27,404 (213%)
7.5%	458,906	34,418 (267%)	57,137 (443%)	49,810 (387%)	33,207 (258%)
8.0%	537,734	43,019 (334%)	68,997 (535%)	60,389 (469%)	40,259 (313%)

Social Security Pays: Single Worker—6,720 (53%)
Couple, Both Spouses Alive—10,080 (79%)
Couple, One Spouse Alive—6,720 (53%)

[1]All figures in constant 1980 dollars, replacement ratios in parentheses.

154

TABLE 14

Maximum Income, Alternative I
Benefits Which Can Be Paid by Private System[1]

Real Rates of Return	Retirement Trust Fund Accumulated at Age 65	Perpetual Annuity	Life Annuity Single Worker	Life Annuity, Couple	
				both spouses alive	one spouse alive
3.0%	482,833	14,485 (21%)	44,020 (62%)	36,687 (52%)	24,458 (34%)
3.5%	550,283	18,260 (27%)	52,149 (73%)	43,721 (62%)	29,147 (41%)
4.0%	623,119	24,925 (35%)	61,313 (86%)	51,696 (73%)	34,464 (48%)
4.5%	703,826	31,672 (45%)	71,829 (100%)	60,892 (85%)	40,595 (57%)
5.0%	794,909	39,745 (56%)	84,055 (117%)	71,628 (100%)	47,752 (67%)
5.5%	898,546	49,420 (69%)	98,349 (137%)	84,225 (118%)	56,150 (79%)
6.0%	1,016,981	61,019 (85%)	115,111 (161%)	99,049 (138%)	66,033 (92%)
6.5%	1,152,743	74,928 (105%)	134,806 (188%)	116,524 (163%)	77,683 (108%)
7.0%	1,308,685	91,608 (128%)	157,980 (220%)	137,151 (191%)	91,434 (128%)
7.5%	1,487,981	111,599 (156%)	185,263 (258%)	161,506 (225%)	107,671 (150%)
8.0%	1,694,603	135,568 (189%)	217,435 (303%)	190,308 (265%)	126,872 (177%)

Social Security Pays: Single Worker—19,076 (27%)
Couple, Both Spouses Alive—28,614 (41%)
Couple, One Spouse Alive—19,076 (27%)

[1]All figures in constant 1980 dollars, replacement ratios in parentheses.

TABLE 15

Average Income, Alternative I
Benefits Which Can Be Paid by Private System[1]

Real Rates of Return	Retirement Trust Fund Accumulated at Age 65	Perpetual Annuity	Life Annuity Single Worker	Life Annuity, Couple	
				both spouses alive	one spouse alive
3.0%	184,241	5,527 (18%)	16,797 (54%)	13,999 (45%)	9,333 (30%)
3.5%	222,331	7,782 (25%)	21,070 (67%)	17,664 (57%)	11,776 (38%)
4.0%	264,549	10,582 (34%)	26,031 (83%)	21,948 (70%)	14,632 (47%)
4.5%	309,383	13,922 (45%)	31,574 (100%)	26,767 (85%)	17,844 (57%)
5.0%	357,535	17,877 (70%)	37,806 (120%)	32,217 (103%)	21,478 (68%)
5.5%	410,964	22,603 (72%)	44,982 (143%)	38,522 (123%)	25,681 (82%)
6.0%	471,492	28,289 (90%)	53,367 (169%)	45,921 (146%)	30,614 (97%)
6.5%	540,865	35,156 (112%)	63,251 (201%)	54,673 (174%)	36,449 (116%)
7.0%	621,068	43,475 (138%)	74,973 (238%)	65,088 (207%)	43,392 (138%)
7.5%	714,027	53,552 (170%)	88,901 (282%)	77,501 (246%)	51,667 (164%)
8.0%	822,083	65,767 (209%)	105,482 (334%)	92,322 (293%)	61,548 (195%)

Social Security Pays: Single Worker—12,816 (40%)
　　　　　　　　　　 Couple, Both Spouses Alive—19,224 (60%)
　　　　　　　　　　 Couple, One Spouse Alive—12,816 (40%)

[1] All figures in constant 1980 dollars, replacement ratios in parentheses.

156

ABOUT THE AUTHOR

Peter J. Ferrara is a graduate of Harvard Law School and Harvard College, where he studied both law and economics. He is an adjunct scholar of the Cato Institute and author of *Social Security: The Inherent Contradiction*. Since writing this monograph, he has become a member of the staff of the White House Office of Policy Development. Previously he had been a New York attorney, specializing in corporate litigation, and Special Assistant to the Assistant Secretary for Policy Development at the Department of Housing and Urban Development, where he was largely responsible for developing the Reagan administration's enterprise zone proposal.

The Cato Institute

The Cato Institute is named for the libertarian pamphlets *Cato's Letters*. Written by John Trenchard and Thomas Gordon, *Cato's Letters* were widely read in the American colonies in the eighteenth century and played a major role in laying the philosophical foundation for the revolution that followed.

The erosion of civil and economic liberties in the modern world has occured in concert with a widening array of social problems. These disturbing developments have resulted from a failure to examine social problems in terms of the fundamental principles of human dignity, economic welfare, freedom, and justice.

The Cato Institute aims to broaden public policy debate by sponsoring programs designed to assist both the scholar and the concerned layperson in analyzing questions of political economy.

The programs of the Cato Institute include the sponsorship and publication of basic research in social philosophy and public policy; publication of the *Cato Journal*, an interdisciplinary journal of public policy analysis, and *Policy Report*, a monthly economic newsletter; "Byline" a daily public affairs radio program; and an extensive program of symposia, seminars, and conferences.

CATO INSTITUTE
224 Second Street SE
Washington, D.C. 20003